Collective Wisdom
in the West

Life Itself

PER
SPEC
TIVA

Introducing Perspectiva Press

Soul food for expert generalists

Perspectiva seeks to understand the relationship between systems, souls and society in a time of crisis, and to develop methods, grounded in an applied philosophy of education, to help us meet the challenges of our time.

As part of this broader endeavour, Perspectiva Press will specialise in short books with occasional longer works. These books will be well-presented and distinctive. Their purpose is to shape and share thinking that helps to:

- create a community of expert generalists with skills of synthesis and epistemic agility

- envisage a world beyond consumerism, and pathways for how we might get there

- support sociological imagination in a dynamic ecological and technological context

- cultivate spiritual sensibility; clarifying how it manifests and why it matters

- encourage a more complex and systemic understanding of the world

- commit to going beyond critique, by developing vision and method

- indicate how we can do pluralism better; epistemic, cultural, political, spiritual

- clarify what it means to become the change we want to see in the world

- develop the authority of people doing important work aligned with Perspectiva

It is unusual for a charity like Perspectiva to become a publisher, even a small one, but we value books as dignified cultural artefacts with their own kind of analogue power, and we believe ideas travel further and connect more deeply when they are rooted in the mandate of a publication designed to last for years, not merely moments. We also see a gap in the market for books that specialise in the kinds of integrative and imaginative sensibilities that speak to the challenges of our time.

Already published:

The World We Create: From god to market *Tomas Björkman*
An entrepreneur offers an historical perspective on achieving a more
meaningful and sustainable world

To be published in 2021:

Unlearn: A compass for radical transformation *Hanno Burmester*
A compass for societal transformation, arising from the personal testimony of
coming out in the shadow of Nazi Germany

**The Entangled Activist: Learning to recognise the master's
tools** *Anthea Lawson*
A seasoned campaigner on how your sense of agency changes when you
realise 'getting the bastards' is not working

The Politics of Waking Up: Power and possibility in the fractal age
Indra Adnan
A psychosocial therapist on refashioning politics by meeting people where they are

**Dispatches from a Time Between Worlds: Crisis and emergence in
metamodernity** *Authors include Jonathan Rowson (ed), Layman Pascal (ed), Zak
Stein, Bonnitta Roy, Daniel Görtz, Lene Rachel Andersen, Sarah Stein Lubrano, Minna
Salami, John Vervaeke and Christopher Mastropietro, Tom Murray, Mark Vernon and
Jonathan Jong, Siva Thambisetty, Jeremy Johnson, Brent Cooper*
An anthology of metamodern scholars and writers on our world-historical
context and pathways to cultural renaissance

In this important and timely book, dense with insight, Liam succeeds where many others have failed, to not only accurately diagnose the root causes of the brokenness that so many of us intuit at the heart of Western scientific materialism, but to indicate the path towards a remedy. Courageously and compassionately teasing apart the roots of our attachments to reason, individuality and equality – notions we would often prefer to take as read, so painful are they to explore – Liam skilfully navigates the reefs and shoals of our reactivity, creating a space for real understanding and a new turning of the wheel of cultural evolution. In this work, Liam models the solution he proposes, by drawing in equal measure on wisdom arising from his own direct, first person meditative investigation, balanced by intellectual rigour and a thorough grasp of developments in neuroscience, psychology and the history and philosophy of science.

Brother Phap Linh, Dharma Teacher, Plum Village Zen Monastery

Liam Kavanagh mobilises brilliantly the insight that attaching to one's sectional or intersectional identity is precisely what wisdom traditions across the world have warned against doing since they began. Such wisdom traditions have earned wide respect in diverse cultures for a reason; Kavanagh extends one's sense of why they are needed. 'Identity politics', whether of the Left or the Right, is a receipt for unwisdom, a guarantor of resentment, anger, incivility and unsatisfactoriness in life; while the path beyond it is a path of freedom. This is a brave and important book for our time, a time when we direly need to find the wisdom to overcome such identities and divisions, and find each other, freely and together.

Professor Rupert Read, former UK national spokesperson for Extinction Rebellion and author of Wittgenstein's Liberatory Philosophy

Collective Wisdom in the West

Beyond the shadows of the Enlightenment

Dr Liam Kavanagh, PhD
Head of Research
Life Itself Institute

Life Itself

Perspectiva Press, London, UK

systems-souls-society.com

First published in 2021

ISBN (POD) 978-1-914568-02-2
ISBN (pbk) 978-1-9998368-1-8
ISBN (ebk) 978-1-9998368-7-0

Cover design Studio Sutherl&

Typeset in Baskerville and Akzidenz Grotesk by www.ShakspeareEditorial.org

Contents

Illustrations

A Preview

THIS BOOK is about how 'enlightened' ideas are contributing to chaos in climate and politics, and how we might get beyond their shadows. About 300 years ago, during the period that we call 'the Enlightenment', usually without irony, we acquired enormously consequential ideas: secularity, the equality of all humans, individualism and the pre-eminence of rationality. Those ideas gradually became 'the truth' while at the same time science gradually realised that no idea is totally in line with the deepest truths. As Buddhists and Stoic philosophers have warned since ancient times, ideas that are out of line with things as they are lead to suffering. Specifically, hardening ideals of rationality, individuality and equality have fed technological hubris, feeble collective action and epidemics of weaponised morality.

I feel the most skilful response is not found in new ideas, but new approaches to ideas. It is easy to say that ideas aren't true; it is hard to break the habit of holding onto them. For this reason, I look for help to Zen Buddhism, whose approach to 'enlightenment' is less about finding perfect ideas, and more about being ready to let go of ideas and keeping them transparent. Ideas are habits that make reality, and admitting our deep addiction to old ways of thinking, some of which we deny we have, and some of which we dare not question, is the first step to going beyond the long shadows cast by our past.

Can we live on cleverness alone?

Many have observed that humans seem *clever* enough to invent technology that opens up a range of choices undreamed of in the past, but not wise enough to choose among these. I examine how influential elites in the West, who have influenced the world, got 'stuck on smart' as a result of pivotal convictions acquired during the Enlightenment that we can see clearly by looking at our own lives rather than travelling back in history. The ability to cultivate and trust intuitions, to be wise, has become impaired by our sense of secularity, and hardened into dogmas by the initial success of rationality, science and capitalism. This leaves us trapped in a mindset that helped to create, and cannot respond to, a family of related crises that threaten the future of our civilisation. I invite the reader to begin undermining this mindset, by contemplating its hold on us.

Looking deeper, collectively

The escalating chaos in climate and politics are just two pieces of evidence, especially dire and incontrovertible, calling us to collectively step back and ask what's wrong. On an individual level, when a person can no longer avoid awareness that there is deep disorder in their life, then, hopefully, they step back and ask what is wrong. Often, it is something close to the core of their being. And after realising this, they often look to their family's past and perhaps the wisdom of their ancestors (such as the Christian tradition or their culture's influential writers). We can do something analogous at the collective level using climate change to 'step back' and look at the trajectory of Western life. Thus, I start with a brief survey of the collective life of Western industrialised civilisation (our collective life), looking for what might have brought us to where we are.

The nearly invisible roots of our crisis

Our historically received ways of imagining the world, of being and acting, have disappeared from awareness as they have become collective habits. The world around us is painted at the speed of thought through our habits of imagination. Reflecting habits, deepened by the seduction of technical solutions that rationality can provide, imagined responses to social difficulties are over-technical in flavour. I write to bring habits alive for readers, into reflective awareness. Postmodern discussions have questioned some of our convictions, especially around rationality, but have not transformed them: for that we need a radically different approach.

Reconnecting to wisdom traditions (connections that we have lost)

Crucially, I focus on the West's loss of connections to the wisdom traditions that our ancestors looked to for guidance in times of crisis. I supplement this discussion by bringing in key insights from Zen Buddhism, a wisdom tradition that is in many ways consistent with the Western value of enquiry that gave birth to the Enlightenment, but which has arrived at very different conclusions regarding the importance of conceptual knowledge, the individual and equality, the three pillars of enlightenment thought. I argue that Zen has much to teach us about how we can question our habitual ways of being and guide ourselves to transformation. Luckily, we don't need to be transformed into scientifically astute buddhas, or anywhere near it, to address our crises. There is a very long way between where we are, now, and the Utopian visions that burst into many readers' minds when spirituality is mentioned alongside politics.[1]

Three attachments of the West: rationality, individuality and equality

Then in the core sections of the book, I examine three particular attachments the West acquired during the Enlightenment: rationality, individuality and equality. These particular ways of looking at life are often seen as 'right' and 'true' rather than simply a perspective. I outline how the hardening of these ideas has impaired our worldview, putting the true nature of things 'in the shadows' at the personal, social and political levels. These attachments are sometimes critically discussed in Western society, but not in the more-than-intellectual way with which we must grapple with bad, stubborn habits before changing them. I discuss many examples, with climate change as a reoccurring theme.

Intended audience

This work is one of many that have made the case for deep cultural change,[2] so I have tried to be brief but broad, to synthesise perspectives and to be accessible as much as to be original. It is meant to be read not only by thinkers, but by people who want to join us at Life Itself in asking how to transform our consciousness and culture in a way appropriate to our civilisational crisis.

At Life Itself we are actively working to create conditions for a wiser future

Though we don't pretend to have the answers fully worked out, I lay out some ways in which Life Itself is already working for greater collective wisdom.

By building communities

For example, we are helping to build communities comprised of people who are both aware of the issues laid out here, and who are drawn to collective heightening of awareness and transformation. We explore possibilities for a culture that puts 'life itself' first – simple appreciation and joy in the moment, and a reflective and interconnected and loving culture, rather than one which is intellectualised, individualist and moralistic. We emphasise how ideas are held (lightly and inquisitively) as much as what our ideas are. We attend with care to our feelings, but seek to avoid being trapped by either thoughts or emotions – to seek real freedom.

Through contemplative activism

We pursue contemplative activism – an activism based on the conviction that our culture's concerns, including climate change, are at least as much 'spiritual' as they are technical in nature. This includes promoting mindful reflection into political and moral questions, promoting scientific enquiry into suffering by testing claims of wisdom traditions, and building self-awareness within the burgeoning cultural change movement. We work to spread awareness, among the many people who are responding to many apparently distinct challenges of our times, that they are in fact responding to the same thing, and we help them to learn from and complement each other.

Introduction

Breaching the barriers to essential conversations

I T IS high time that we as a society deeply grapple with the truth behind statements that our society is technologically capable, analytically sophisticated and yet very unwise. A small army of our greatest minds offer quotes like the following:

certainly we should take care not to make the intellect our god; it has, of course, powerful muscles, but no personality. It cannot lead, it can only serve; and it is not fastidious in its choices of a leader. This characteristic is reflected in the qualities of its priests, the intellectuals. The intellect has a sharp eye for methods and tools, but is blind to ends and values. So it is no wonder that this fatal blindness is handed from old to young and today involves a whole generation.

Albert Einstein[3]

Modern bourgeois society ... a society that has conjured up such gigantic means of production and of exchange, is like the sorcerer, who is no longer able to control the powers of the nether world whom he has called up by his spells.

Karl Marx (not talking about climate change)[4]

The end of the human race will be that it will eventually die of civilization.

attributed to Ralph Waldo Emerson

Ultimately, there may be intelligences on the horizon that we don't even know about .... One candidate that has emerged for consideration is spiritual or moral intelligence

Thomas Armstrong[5]

In our search for knowledge, in our acquisitive desires, we are losing love, we are blunting the feeling for beauty, the sensitivity to cruelty ... if the mind and heart are suffocated by knowledge, and if the cause of suffering is explained away, life becomes vain and meaningless.

J. Krishnamurti[6]

Such remarks have been nodded at for centuries, but Westerners, and humans generally, are still not a self-possessed group choosing its future in a considered fashion. Instead, we are dangerously misguided, under the control of old habits. Now is the time to do something about it – not only because information spreads far faster than ever before, not only because of the urgent climate crisis, but because it gets harder every day for us to collectively deny that radical changes are necessary. The main impediments to the necessary conversations – denial, and fear of ostracism for breaking cultural taboos – are falling away. The change required will be both culturally redefining and historically significant.

There are plenty of hang-ups that we still need to get past on our way to greater collective wisdom. We worry that, if we name wise or foolish ways of being, we'll be seen as invalidating other's choices (is materialism unwise? What about believing in the afterlife?). If we look for consensus on wisdom, we threaten others' precious individual and equal exercise of free choice. People who dare talk about wisdom get called hippies or hypocrites, and issues of collective wisdom quickly get into territory marked with the red warning labels of 'new-age', 'political', 'religious' and 'moralistic'. If we can't talk about essential matters together, though, extreme incoordination and self-organisation into insular camps (within which important matters are discussed) are inevitable.

Further, the idea that a person's actions can be a meaningful part of culture change or politics has often been ridiculed reflexively as delusional, or even childish, for decades. We all know the familiar situation – conversation turns to the big picture, and immediately ironic remarks start about saving the world and regressing to college. In the last few years, though, we've been treated to the sight of the world's leaders being humiliatingly hectored by a teenage girl (Greta Thunberg), who inspires hero worship by adults worldwide because she talks about what is important. Her voice stands out now, because in the past, it was somehow decided that questioning the way the world is working is an adolescent's activity. Is there any wonder we feel a little bit lost?

However, an adult who feels the urge to look at the big picture can suddenly find many conversation partners – on the internet or in subcultures. This book is a humble offering to these 'echo chambers', which I hope grow larger and more influential than either those of the sixties – which still haunt our memories with what might have been, or those of the salons of Paris – which remade our culture and whose conversations still echo today.

Definitions of key terms

In this section, I'll follow the convention of defining pivotal terms, such as *wisdom* and *collective*. But not without a warning: as I see it, Western culture's habit of grasping after precise definitions is an everyday symptom of our profoundest source of unwisdom, an addiction to certainty and control. I will try my best to add just enough definition to my terms while not grasping for an impossible level of precision.

The allure and danger of definition seeking

Before continuing, it is worth contemplating the drive for precise definitions. When we can find them, precise definitions are great – but it's hard not to notice that they usually elude us. As the great physicist Richard Feynman said:

> We can't define anything precisely. If we attempt to,
> we get into that paralysis of thought that comes to
> philosophers … one saying to the other: 'you don't know
> what you are talking about!' The second one says: 'what
> do you mean by talking? What do you mean by you?
> What do you mean by know?'[7]

Cognitive psychology has agreed with Feynman for decades, showing that human intuitions about whether objects should be called tables, chairs or just about anything cannot be captured with great verbal precision, such as by listing the traits or functions an object must have in order to be called a 'table'. Words are imprecise because they are the way we try to grasp the large and chaotic universe with a 1.4 kilo human brain. We have a small number of words with which we must talk and think about the vastly greater number of things that there are in the world.

Precise definitions can mostly be found for categories whose sole function is to be part of a man-made intellectual system such as 'citizen', which is part of the legal system, or 'negative real number', which is part of the mathematical system. There are a few precise concepts that really seem to capture a 'natural kind' of thing, a kind that exists independently of the human intellect. Examples are 'electron' and 'hydrogen atom' from the physical sciences.[8] But when we try to define things we actually see in daily life, invariably containing huge swarms of interrelating atoms, definitions get quite fuzzy. There is a wondrous infinity of things that can be made out of tiny atoms and we have but a few words with which to talk about them. It is a miracle that we can make sense of anything at all, and by expecting precise definitions, maybe we are getting a little greedy.

At some level, I feel, most of us know this. Why are many still drawn towards precise definitions? Because if something could be defined precisely, it would be easier to understand precisely and control precisely. Coming to a recurring point of the book, it is good to consider whether we expect precise definitions because there is good reason to believe they are possible, or because they'd be nice to have.

Adding definition to the notion of wisdom

If we understand wisdom precisely, we'd have an answer for everything. This is because 'wisdom' can be loosely defined as the ability to make appropriate responses – especially in contexts that are changing, subtle or confusing. An 'appropriate response' is one that is consistent with our primal urge to flourish. 'To flourish' basically means to enjoy life *as a whole*, with all its difficulties: being happy, hard to beat down, engaged, healthy and vigorous, and to allow others and our descendants to do the same.

This may sound too vague, but actually it isn't *that* vague. The distinction between enjoyable (positive, pleasing) and (negative, unpleasing) sensations is easy to understand, and so is the idea of finding a balance of experiences that is as enjoyable as possible over the long run. This definition may not satisfy some, though, because it doesn't say how we can flourish, *how* we can be wise across many contexts.

My judgement is that trying to add *that* much definition would be overambitious at this stage, but it is helpful to distinguish wisdom from the related term *cleverness*. A well-known distinction is that 'cleverness' entails pursuing goals effectively, while 'wisdom' entails adopting goals that lead to flourishing.

We can illustrate this distinction by example: we can conceive of a clever tabloid journalist, but a wise, flourishing tabloid journalist is a very counterintuitive notion. The same is true of pornographers, big-game hunters, prize-fighters, heroin dealers and pimps. Most people would admit that to excel in these professions, it helps to be clever, while also feeling that choosing such pursuits was unwise. We may suspect that clever heroin dealers and pimps got where they are by becoming sort of ensnared in a certain way of being – enslaved to certain drives and desires, to prides or to badly chosen friendships somewhere along the way. Seeing past such traps and finding our way out of them is part of wisdom.

On the other hand, if we are told a prize-fighter's story, we might suddenly see him as wise. He could have been gifted with few opportunities in a rough life, but had a talent for fighting and a need to support a family, and could have retired young with his wits about him. Perhaps he negotiated his challenging context pretty well. The point is, if we grasp too tightly at what we know, we can sometimes fail to see wisdom.

This brings us to another crucial point: the words 'wise' or 'clever' seem to be set apart by the way of being that underlies them. Cleverness is more associated with calculation, while wisdom more reflects a deep and well-honed sense of what is right and of integrity, a carefully cultivated way of seeing. We are more likely to call a person wise if they make an appropriate response, guided by a difficult-to-explain sense of what is right, rather than by 'figuring something out'. Imagine, for example, two people who bought the same reliable, eco-friendly car: one did a statistical analysis of lifetime costs; the second found that a reliable car fits with a deep commitment to not being wasteful. We have more of a tendency to call the second wise and the first clever. This shows our intuitive understanding that wisdom often comes from a felt sense that is informed by deep principles. This is the sort of knowledge we rely on more when we face contexts that are highly complex, changing and subtle.

I am still not getting very specific by saying that wisdom reflects a cultivated felt sense of what will allow us to flourish, which in turn relies on cultivation of insight and integrity. But it is worth asking: 'what would a precise definition of wisdom look like?' To be more precise, a definition would have to say what kinds of actions are wise rather than what kinds of results are wise. And that would require saying something very general about what kinds of actions lead to what kinds of results. But the relation between actions and results depends on contexts, and there are too many contexts to name. So, if I go further, I would no longer be offering a simple definition that clarifies the subject of this book's discussion, but offering a rather grand theory of flourishing.

I will end my offer of greater definition, here, well short of a precise definition. I feel that discussing how to flourish despite our particular culture's challenges is more useful than a grand theory. But to lead into that discussion, I will briefly mention something that both scientists and mystics would agree is a general characteristic of wise people. Wise people use their feelings, intuitions, perceptions, memories and ideas without being a slave to them. Essentially, this means that we let go of ideas formed in one context, always in the past, often quite different from the context we are in, when these no longer serve us. If we are in crisis, we might want to consider that views which no longer serve us have gotten us there. To find out what views might be causing us suffering, we should look at those we hold most closely, that are central to the sense we make of the world. Much of this book argues that historically recent glorification of rationality, individualism and even equality are views that need to be reassessed.

Adding definition to the notion of *collective* wisdom

But what is *collective wisdom*? Collective Wisdom has a metaphorical element, drawing a parallel from an individual life to a wider collective. Wisdom is measured by action and so a collective worth writing about is one that does or at least could act together. The collectives that write laws, build schools and healthcare systems, and that haven't done very much about climate change together, are the collectives that have a chance to collectively create sustainable well-being.

Who or what are the collectives that are being wise or unwise? The collectives that I have written about here are quite broad; they are the collectives that make up 'the West', which basically means the societies whose major cultural influences can be traced to Western Europe. It is not the only collective worth writing about, but it is a collective of which I am part, composed of people and countries that I feel are misguided in similar, deeply concerning ways. The main focus of the book is on deeply rooted cultural attachments or assumptions, which are central to how we conceive of 'the West', and central to how it thinks and acts. To presage one major point of the book, the unwise perspective of extreme individualism has made the West into collectives that have a tendency to deny the collective nature of human life.

Subjectivity

The definition of wisdom offered above might sound subjective – *it is*, and it should be. The subjective is important even though it is not precise. Subjective intuitions guide us, moment by moment, through complexity. Also, what makes life worth living or not living is the quality of our subjective experience, including not only simple pleasures but also meaning, aspiration and caring for others. Flourishing has a lot to do with subjectively feeling good, and not feeling bad – good feelings are reinforcing for our behaviour, while bad feelings are discouraging. Good feelings are an end, but also a means to this end – a sign we can follow that says we are on the way to doing something that 'makes sense' for us (is there a difference between a sense and a feeling?) Good subjective feelings and a lack of bad feelings often indicate that our minds, conditioned on an unfathomable amount of evolutionary experience (of our animal as well as human ancestors) approve of what is happening. Generating good feelings isn't a straightforward process though – it is easy to grasp at good feelings and come away with bad ones (for example, the search for impossible precision, as above). Usually, though, a bad feeling on the fringe of consciousness is ignored during a failed grab at happiness.

Consider how feelings guide us in choosing whether to use a word like 'wise' to describe an action. It feels 'right' to use wisdom to describe an action that will increase the long-term well-being of ourselves and others. It may feel 'good' to describe oneself as wise, as we get the warm, pleasant sensations of pride, but it often may not feel 'right'.

There might be a nagging feeling alongside the pride that we have to ignore in order to feel good. This annoying feeling may be there because we know we have much to learn and sense that we are calling ourselves wise inauthentically, or out of a need to put ourselves above others. Describing things in a way that 'feels right' is a subjective process. We are not simply guided by feeling pride, but by feeling an absence of conflict or shame, and by an impulse towards feeling whole or integrous.

Doing the right thing also feels good, just not in the same way that orgasms, greasy red meat and chocolate feel good. These are all examples that people use to argue that pursuing pleasure and avoiding pain is very different from wisdom – but we ignore nagging fringe feelings in order to pursue such pleasures. There are always good feelings when we have an orgasm, but, as a whole, our state of mind is better when we *feel right* about the orgasm. Guilt and worry about playing with others' or one's own feelings are often ignored during casual sex. Unpleasant moral and health concerns are often ignored while eating red meat, like the nagging knowledge that a heavy feeling and low energy may soon result. When we consume lots of chocolate, this comes with the knowledge that we're going to have to lie down after a sugar spike (chocolate is a relatively wise vice).

Wisdom itself is the ability to sense our way to flourishing, a sustainable joy that comes more naturally when we don't ignore sensations 'in the back of our mind', at the fringes of our consciousness. Sensations that tend to guide us to wise actions include feelings of wholeness and integrity, of joy, meaning, vigour, alertness and healthiness. On the other hand, feelings that indicate we risk taking the wrong path include inner conflict, aversiveness, sloth, 'cloudiness' and so on.

It is worth mentioning that good feelings are, nowadays, an especially problematic guide to wise actions, even if they are often the best guide we have. Our environment is one we've made for each other while operating largely under the curious assumption that open economic rivalry between people produces the best collective outcomes 'as if guided by an invisible hand'.[9] We must navigate an environment full of an increasing number of hacks of our biology: alcohol has been joined by new drugs, computer games, infinite pornography and so on. These temptations are often profitable for their inventors, and have a life of their own, proliferating themselves by muddling our felt sense of what is valuable. All of this complicates our efforts to sense which, of the many ways of seeing the world, being in it and acting, will *really* be useful. But if ways of thinking and acting can 'sustainably' give good feelings, over very long periods of time, to many people, then they are probably wise.

All generalisation is not over-generalisation

In this book, I will sometimes talk about 'us' as a society or a civilisation. Some people may dislike this, believing that generalisation necessarily implies disrespect for diversity. For example, despite the West's general unwisdom there are many good things in our society. Our hopes for navigating our current situation are tied to the wisdom of some of our contemporaries and ancestors. However, generalisations are impossible to avoid, especially in a book about *collective* wisdom. Despite millions of individual exceptions to general unwisdom, there are not enough, yet, to give most of us deep faith in the future.

The idea of avoiding generalisations has become fashionable as an attempt to reject the very same overreach of reason that drives our stubborn search for definitions. The person who badly wants a perfect theory or precise definition will deny exceptions to his definition, preserving his feeling of having things 'nailed down'. This is annoying, but the claim that 'you can't generalise' is often a reflexive reaction to the fear of *over*-generalisation. Automatic reactions against anything make us less, rather than more free.

The simplest use of language depends on broad generalisations, and it always will while humans are using our small brains to describe a big world. Unfortunately, that's the difficult situation that we are in. For instance, the word 'French' means nothing unless there is greater similarity among French people than there is among humans, generally

– otherwise we wouldn't talk about French people, but just people. Woman is a generalisation and so is man, and so are transgender and +. There is no number of words/generalisations that will do complete justice to all individuals, though we can always do better. Not even eight billion words would do, because people change and adapt to situations every moment, and humans on average have 30,000 at their disposal. If we are to talk about the issues that affect all of these lives, we must accept that the question is not whether to generalise, but how to hold our generalisations skilfully.

1 Will Climate Change Cause Us to Wise Up, Finally?

MAN-MADE CLIMATE change (which I will just call 'climate change', following convention) is a powerful means of staring our collectively inadequate wisdom in the face. Enough has been said about climate change that you might be sick of hearing about it. But just consider: we *still* have no credible collective agreements on how to respond to climate change – even now, with the Arctic ice cap rapidly disappearing, droughts beginning to disrupt agriculture and our food supply,[10] and with scientists having been so worried, for years, that they are afraid to voice their personal fears publicly, for fear of starting a general panic.[11]

Despite all that, the climate situation is still not widely seen as a major threat to the existence of our civilisation. What could be more collectively unwise? And even if the level of threat was 'concerning but nothing to panic over' (as many think), climate change would still demonstrate that our collective wisdom is inadequate to the demands placed on it. We could have changed our carbon-based economy years ago, but we didn't. The job has become harder and harder every year.

But the threat is worse than almost any 'mainstream' group, including educated elites, has accepted, showing that blindness extends to every level.[12] The climate science community accepts that it made an enormous error when setting early emissions targets which aimed to limit global temperature rises to 2°C.[13] Current science shows that a 2°C rise will probably destabilise the Earth's climate system in ways which will be very difficult to adjust to.[14] To take one example, the Arctic region is quickly thawing, which creates concerning follow-on effects, such as the loss of massive ice sheets that reflect light (and thus, heat), as well as huge releases of greenhouse gases from thawing biological matter that has been stored for millennia in permafrost. There will soon be a moment just like the one where we realised that all those World Health Organization warnings about the coronavirus were real, except it will be about climate.

There are many other ways in which our unwisdom could be demonstrated, but the slow change of the Earth's climate may be grave enough to break the inertia that has prevented serious conversation about wiser societies. Man-made climate change also features in this book because people have heard a lot about climate change. This allows me to mostly skip the facts and figures – and I will.

I want to emphasise that we are now continuously disrupting our surroundings through innovation, and this will bring more challenges. That is why this book is not about addressing climate change, but what we can do to become the kinds of societies that would have averted the climate change crisis earlier. For instance, this piece was largely written before the Covid crisis hit, and the response to Covid reflects the same pre-existing conditions described below.[15] However, Covid does not pose the same threat as climate change, and has not proven to be beyond our capacity to address over decades. Climate change is still in the news after 30 years because we have mistakenly had faith that we could invent ideas that could solve it, because we are too individualistic to come to collective agreements, and because our politics are too dysfunctional to address it, as discussed in greater length below. Similar things could be said about other aspects of ecocide (e.g. biodiversity loss), but climate change is the wake-up call we are having the hardest time ignoring.

Climate also demonstrates that greed and selfishness alone cannot explain our crisis. We have talked a lot lately about the disproportionate influence of rich white males, but climate change cannot be understood *solely* as part of the age-old story of powerful groups protecting their influence (of course this plays a role). The age-old desire of the privileged to hold on to what they have *might* totally explain some of our problems: huge disparities in income, and perhaps the rise of Donald Trump and nationalist governments.[16] But almost nobody, and certainly nobody's children, will be privileged enough to be better off after an environmental collapse. There must be a deep delusion at the root of the climate emergency.

Climate change became the climate *crisis* because of a sustained collective failure to question and make sense of the big picture. For years, nobody imagined or debated the possibilities for a different society because nobody else was talking about new big visions. Changing the big picture requires lots of people, and since not enough people were even reflecting on the possibility for change, most individuals felt that trying to achieve change was a waste of time. Television and looking at social media seemed like better uses of free time. Maybe you can remember conversations, like the many that I've had, at gatherings of friends that veered towards this big picture and ended with the downbeat conclusion that nothing will change until a time of crisis. However, enough people are beginning to sense that we are at such a point that it is possible to start real reflection, deep and widespread enough to feed the movement towards collective change.

The question is, how did we get here? Let's take a step back and let our collective life flash before our eyes.

2 A Contemplation of a Few Key Elements of Western History

I N ORDER to set up a discussion of knowing ourselves, I'd like to reconsider a few elements of Western history that are well known, but not well enough considered. If they were well considered *enough*, then we'd probably behave differently.

Money and consumption

The most ostentatious characteristic of our society, as has been observed constantly for centuries, is its focus on money and consumption. I will say only a few short words about these issues, because they are so often discussed elsewhere.

What is truly remarkable about money and consumption is how strongly we claim to know that money and consumption are not the route to well-being or happiness in our lives, and how much we remain in their thrall. This is a lot like an addict's inability to give up a drug, a point I'll return to later. But first we can briefly let our well-known consumerist habits into our awareness.

The spread of liberal democracy as a spread of merchant values and priorities

Today's dominant political order began when a new group, who had declared themselves fit to vote, wrestled away the king's inherited right to rule. This group was led, for the most part, by rich and well-resourced (and male) merchants. Similar classes of people had existed for a very long time in many places, but in England and other European countries they were powerful enough to take control of the government, and able to build an ideology that worked to keep them in power.

In both the US and Britain, and other early democracies, this group set up an economic and social system in which their merchant values (making lots of money) were strongly reflected in collective choices. The interests of business have, over time, heavily influenced all manner of legislation, schooling priorities and choices to engage in foreign wars and create empires.

One result has been rich societies that emphasised material acquisition and production. These societies met their material needs and exceeded them by technical innovation and wars. These moved to become consumerist societies, in which people drew their pleasure from having produced products that they have no connection to, and distinguished themselves socially by consumption. A simultaneous turn away from wisdom traditions (see below) exacerbated this movement.

The famous curve in Figure 1 shows the most optimistic view of the relationship between happiness and income that any researcher endorses (more on the objections below). Simple plots of income against average happiness from various countries show that additional material resources do make one happier when we are quite poor. It makes sense that meeting basic biological needs makes it easier to enjoy life. Though there are millions of people within industrialised countries who suffer from a lack of material resources, basic needs stopped being the main driver of consumption growth in the West long ago.

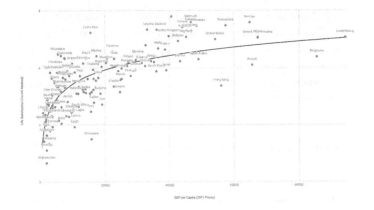

Figure 1 GDP per Capita v. Life Satisfaction, 2017 (source: World Bank)

A logarithmic relationship between life satisfaction and income is suggested by a simple plot of GDP per capita and life satisfaction across a sample of nations. This has been observed within countries by many economists, notably Wolfers and Stevenson.[17] Note the relationship is plotted on a linear scale.[18] The left vertical axis shows self-reported life satisfaction on a scale ranging from 0 to 10 where 10 is the highest possible life satisfaction. The horizontal axis represents annual income in 2011 US dollars.

We have now started travelling farther along the flatter part of this curve, which would have to go all the way out to 1.1 million dollars a year to reach nine. Making this available to everybody on earth would mean incomes 15 times the size of the average US citizen's, which is not a realistic goal anytime soon – the planet's ecosystems would collapse first. Even if we were to accept the controversial idea that the few very rich people within our societies are made very happy by their possessions, it is impossible for Western societies to get much happier, as a whole, by pursuing greater incomes.

Our continued collective pursuit of higher incomes shows that our relation to consumption as a whole is a mass psychological addiction.

An addiction is simply a habit that resists being broken, though it is obviously detrimental, in the eyes of either the addict himself or his society.[19] Many of us wish we could break a compulsion to have more things, knowing that we are fatter, more jealous, less healthy, busier and more distracted than we need to be. But we just can't seem to do it; we are surrounded by enablers, and our drives have been well fed.

I will discuss later how this situation calls for re-engagement with wisdom traditions that have traditionally dealt with habits of mind that we would rather not have, specifically acquisitiveness and hedonism. For now, I will simply note that many of the most effective methods of addiction treatment (such as Alcoholics Anonymous) have a 'spiritual element'.[20]

Culture and habits of consumption

After discussing our consumption habits, authors often suggest that we should measure ourselves against gross domestic happiness (GDH) rather than GDP. Of course, a wise society would probably do something like this, but adopting these national standards will not make a wise society. Compiling GDH is worth doing, and arguing for it is worth doing, but without a change in culture, making an official commitment to pursue GDH is just another collective New Year's resolution.

I contend that GDP reflects, rather than makes, a culture. GDP is just the sum of individual incomes, and so it is the natural measure of success for a money-focused society. An ideology has formed around this which makes economic growth synonymous with 'progress', reflecting an addiction to money and status. This ideology is most deep-rooted and influential in the United States and the United Kingdom, it was already well entrenched in the former when the French writer Alexis De Tocqueville documented it on his famed 1831 tour of the US and has been an unbroken tradition since then.[21]

Since the rise of the merchant class to power, status has largely become more closely connected to money. Status-seeking, generally, is a matter of fighting for a slice of a pie whose size doesn't change, no matter what we do collectively. To the extent that economic activity is driven by status-seeking it gives us nothing as a society. The never-ending race for status often drives consumption more than the pleasure of consumption itself, but it adds to environmental degradation just the same.

Racism, nationalism and colonialism

The brutal construction of colonial empires and slaveholding practices, driven by wills to riches and to collective and personal power over others, and enabled by advancing technology are the most infamous aspects of Western history. This is a legacy that still affects the lives of millions of citizens who suffer from racism and unequal treatment under the criminal justice system in Western countries, or billions who live in nations born out of colonial legacies under regimes often maintained by subtler forms of imperialism. It has a way of remaining awkwardly in a dark shadow, though it is too large to be hidden, with light cast upon it in brief flashes, such as after the killing of George Floyd by police in Minneapolis.

The arc of this long story could be told very simply: a period of technological superiority gave the West power, which it abused on a massive scale. So, a lot of people, especially very powerful ones, would like to hide or forget about these aspects of the present and past and their implications for the self-image of Western societies. The full story is of course complex and much written about, but these many words have been unable to bring the past fully enough to light to be truly reckoned with. Perhaps this is a timeless situation: power will be around as long as humans have a capacity for it, and denial of its effects on others will be around as long as we have capacity for love. Where this book might add a little to this story is in discussing how Western attachments to Enlightenment ideas are intertwined with empire and racism and our denial of it. So, I will return to discussion of this deep shadow later on, after reflecting on equality.

The rise of secularity

Another distinctive feature of Western society is the marginalisation of what we would call religious matters in public life. This is the direct result of both the dogmatic and oppressive form that institutional Christianity took, and the rise of rationality and science (discussed in the next section). In practice, this has meant something of a taboo around the idea of 'spiritual guidance' and the legitimacy of acting on this. Privately, of course, many heads of state and major corporations as well as 'normal folks' rely on this guidance, and it is intertwined with the artistic impulse. But however important it is, it is not something we can expect to discuss openly while remaining respectable.

In order to understand this issue, we must first understand the word 'religion'. This word traditionally refers to things that Westerners understand by analogy to Christianity. Christianity is the only religion that Westerners have traditionally had some experience with, and they understand other religions as other people's version of Christianity. For the related traditions of Islam and Judaism, this concept works relatively well, and people who come from within those three traditions can somehow understand each other if each group grounds their own concept of religion in their particular tradition (e.g. Muslims can also think of Christianity as what Christians have instead of Islam, and achieve a useful but imperfect understanding). Buddhism, Hinduism and Animism are not well understood this way.

By wisdom tradition, I mean a tradition of practices and thought that is relied on in order to decide what is important and to make the broadest and deepest choices in life – what is 'good' or 'a life well lived', what is right and wrong and so on.

Many, if not all, wisdom traditions do not sit comfortably with discussions in Western public life because they share with Christianity a reliance on and cultivation of 'spiritual guidance' and a belief that we can and must use this to find out the deepest and most meaningful truths. They do not bow to rationality. Those wisdom traditions which have been labelled 'religions' usually have rituals and procedures that do not appear to serve a rational purpose.

Rational questioning of tradition-derived religious authority drove much of the Enlightenment and remade our culture. Religious authorities justified what they did based on refined inner guidance, often of somebody (usually dead) in a position of (supposed) authority. As science has become the arbiter of truth, religious authorities have often been viewed as tragically misguided or even sinister with burdensome power over humans' lives. The Christian traditions, with their belief in an afterlife and divine intervention, and in some cases sceptres and sacraments for transforming water into wine and wafers into flesh have come for many, and especially the elite educated class, to be a symbol of hollow pomp, wishful thinking, superstition and arbitrary authority.

In the West, the damage caused by authoritarian arrogance in Christianity fatally undermined not only organised religion, but also the legitimacy of citing one's private inner life as justification for beliefs and actions. Religions which had been embarrassed by scandal and science had, after all, justified themselves by citing the experiences of Jesus, the prophets and their supposed successors, the popes. The result has been a taboo around discussing religion or guidance in social situations. Our Christian past may have contributed to the belief in human dignity and universal brotherhood that powered many of the Enlightenment's successes, but its non-intellectual elements of group practice, silence, prayer and transcendent truth have mainly been ignored – or even ridiculed – in intellectual circles as their value is hard to grasp, and the authority derived from them appears prone to abuse (see next section).

The solution that we have agreed upon is simply not to talk about the territory covered by religions in public life. The separation of inner guidance and public behaviour is not possible, however, and their lack of discussion of wisdom traditions in public life has slowly eroded their vitality.

Guidance and its demise

What is guidance?

At this point, I must introduce the notion of 'guidance', and discuss the decline of its reputation in the West.[22] Guidance is what I will call that ability which gives us a felt sense of direction or inspiration about what to do, without always explaining to us why. It might seem simpler to use the word 'intuition', but I've chosen 'guidance' because intuition is often equated with snap judgements. By 'guidance' I mean an extended process of hearing and working with one's inner sense of direction, allowing intuitions to form, questioning intuitions and getting new intuitions. It is often described as a conversation with one's true self, or one's 'soul', or with God. Many, including myself, would agree that the sense of direction during both meditation and prayer often comes from the same sense, which I call guidance. My experience is that most people who count themselves as 'spiritual' agree with what I say about this sense while having very different names for it, and different stories about its ultimate source.[23]

Our culture finds guidance problematic because it is often not easy to justify or explain in words. People who feel guided by considered engagement with their intuitions often simply get an irresistible feeling that they should do something. If guidance is more related to the work of an artistic or musical creation than to an accountant's creation of a balance sheet, its elusive nature should not be surprising. But guidance is frustratingly subjective, at least to a culture that has become used to the idea that there are clear answers to life's important questions.

One way of using the word contemplation is 'engaging with our guidance' rather than thinking, in order to get a sense of something. For example, when we are *thinking* about a career change, we are more likely to be working through costs and benefits based on what we know, already. When we are *contemplating* a career change, we work slowly and mindfully with our intuitions (feelings of guidance), allowing them to take a certain course that, eventually, results in a feeling of clarity in our actions. Another name might be 'looking deeply' and acting on what we hear.

If we just examine some simple statements about guidance, we can see why thorny issues continually arise:

A. It gives a sense of how to act but often no explanation of why.

B. It is not perfect, but can be honed: some people have cultivated their guidance more than others.

C. It is built by examining our feelings closely and questioning them.

D. Guidance typically comes to a quiet and concentrated mind capable of sensing complex inner feelings, not to one that is full of rushing thoughts.

E. Over time others can see that a person's guidance takes them to good results.

F. People who have worked on their guidance are better able to appreciate the guidance of others.

G. There are subjective experiences of guidance that we can talk about, that mean little to a person who has not experienced something similar.

These characteristics make it difficult for people who rely on guidance to justify themselves to each other logically or to create consensus by sharing their experiences. They also tend to result in people listening to well-guided authorities without expecting much explanation, which creates opportunities for abuse.

The tendency of wisdom traditions to decay

It is widely noted that there is a tendency in wisdom traditions to slowly collapse into dogma – grasping at forms that are visible and that can be grasped onto, rather than cultivation of the invisible interior life. As the ancient book of Tao states:

> Failing Tao, man resorts to Virtue. Failing Virtue, man
> resorts to humanity. Failing humanity, man resorts to
> morality. Failing morality, man resorts to ceremony. Now,
> ceremony is the merest husk of faith and loyalty; It is the
> beginning of all confusion and disorder (Chapter 38)

The tradition is then sometimes renewed by a person who can clearly see what is wrong with a degraded tradition and acquire enough confidence of others that they can do something about it, which often requires speaking with clarity, conviction and charisma (such people are called 'renewers').

Wisdom traditions, which are supposed to be storehouses of what has been found by inner guidance, also often descend into superstition, lies, empty ritual and control.

There are a number of good reasons why all this might happen:

1. Guidance is hard to communicate: it is easy for us to misunderstand the words of well-guided others, who are describing an inner life we have not experienced.

2. It is easy to mistake delusive or dishonest people for well-guided 'spiritual masters'.

3. Supposed masters might pass on foolishness because they delude themselves about their mastery, and such delusional people can still be very charismatic.[24]

4. There is no such thing as guidance.

We have moved towards the last explanation in the contemporary West, though almost all other cultures across the world and throughout time focus on the other reasons. This move is among the greatest sources of our problems, and is aided by a distorted faith in our ability to explain useful actions, as will be discussed later on.

The arts are one area where the importance of guidance remains uncontroversial, and artistic experience backs up point 1, showing the difficulty of transmitting guidance. Music, poetry and visual art act as mediums for developing, communicating and expressing an inner reality in ways that conventional words cannot. Interpretations and reactions to these arts vary, and what sense we make of an artist or poet is highly variable.

Just as expressed in point 2, these dynamics lead to widespread agreement that there are a large number of artistic geniuses and charlatans who are given equal respect by the public. Wisdom traditions imply that sayings stemming from guidance are often misunderstood in a similar fashion. For example, early Buddhist tracts show the Buddha constantly correcting potentially dangerous misunderstandings of things that he said, and arguments over the meanings of scripture are many.

We can get some understanding of how so much self-delusion and misunderstanding can arise by considering the phenomenon of *overimitation*, which has been documented by psychologists. People who do not understand how a certain action really works tend to imitate unimportant details of others' actions. For example, children with no experience with light switches will turn on a light switch by pressing it with their head if they see an adult turn the light switch on in this way. Turning the switch on with their hand would be easier, and that is what older children with greater understanding do.[25] Likewise, imitation of form is the instinctive move of a person who wants to learn wisdom (guidance) that is currently beyond them (they are not yet able to relate their inner life to that of their teacher). This means repeating words, expressions and gestures and showing the serenity of a master, but the inner invisible way of being may elude such a person.

People who imitate or fake actions can sometimes fool themselves and others into thinking that their inner life is similar to that of a master – which, after all, the imitators know nothing about. That is, a person who 'performs serenity' can tell themselves that in fact they are basically serene because their actions are the same actions as those of a serene person, and ignore their tumultuous inner life.

Finally, both points 2 and 3 are made plausible by the high temptations towards charlatanism in professions that rely on guidance. If the guidance of the public is not developed, and so they cannot confidently check a supposed master's words against their own guidance, then claiming to be better guided represents an easy way to achieve social position, respect and money. Obviously, Christianity accepts this – Jesus famously said: 'Beware of false prophets, who come to you in sheep's clothing but inwardly are ravenous wolves.'

The point is that, if the nature of guidance was exactly as summarised in the simple statements above, there would still be charlatans who would claim guidance, as well as deluded prophets who have falsely convinced themselves of their deep guidance. There would also be teachers who actually understood something. However, people, especially inexperienced people, would have a hard time saying who was who.

A well-prepared fall from grace

Wisdom traditions around the world have fallen prey to some of these dynamics and been led periodically by fools and charlatans. However, European Christianity and especially the Catholic Church of the Dark Ages, created an especially elaborate and effective method of claiming an incontestable monopoly on inner guidance on many subjects.[26] As in many cultures, the Catholic mythology held that our personal guidance is sometimes influenced by God, but clergy claimed a nearly exclusive ability to hear God most clearly, with the Pope having perfect guidance from God on many crucial subjects.[27] To sum it up succinctly, spirituality and art were certainly in the Church's exclusive domain, but the borders of these domains were fuzzy, different from contemporary norms and dependent on political squabbles with monarchs. We all know that Earth's position in the Cosmos, for example, was a matter of papal authority, but so too were all manner of moral questions.

The Church offered the common person little opportunity to cultivate their own 'divine' guidance, offering services in a language (Latin) that commoners did not understand. It upheld its spiritual authority, not with moral beauty, but with grand symbolism (supposedly, ornate churches were outward evidence of the church's divine guidance). It focused teachings on claims to rewards in the afterlife, and used its perceived monopoly on guidance to control public life in dysfunctional ways, using excommunication, demanding indulgences for political reasons and allowing high-ranking clergy to maintain large numbers of sexual servants.[28] In short, it cynically built an undeserved claim to guidance and exploited this monopoly to an incredible extent.[29]

The rise of rationality and science

The rise of rationality and science explains much of the demise of spirituality in the West. Rationality met a troubled Christian wisdom tradition, and produced such mind-boggling results, in terms of material wealth and happiness, and overturning of dogma, that it has been thought it could displace guidance in general.

Justification of ideas by either one's own intuition, or that of another, played a far greater role in culture until science came about. Reason and logic had been around for a long time, but were of limited use in understanding the world. What really changed things was the experiment. During the European renaissance, the wealth gathered by successful merchants allowed them independence from the Church and allowed more people to spend time understanding the world through reading secular texts that made their way into Europe through the Middle East, thinking, and arguing. There began to be revived interest in ancient Greek and Roman, and in Arabian, thinkers, but with a new advance – instead of arguing points solely through elaborate arguments or by relying on their own guidance, or that of spiritual authorities, people started to look at whether an idea fit with observations of the world. They kept ideas that fit the world and threw out the ones that did not. Rather than trying to argue their case based on shared facts, scientists started going out and getting better facts.

This process started humbly enough, with Galileo dropping objects off the tower of Pisa in order to determine whether heavier objects fell faster than lighter ones. People thought that heavier objects fell faster, but it turned out that everything fell at the same speed, settling the arguments. Initial experiments created evidence and observations to measure ideas against, and theories such as Newton's ideas about gravity were created. They burst into a world of mystery where little was understood systematically. The knowledge attained about physical objects, the first subject of science, was remarkable. So, we decided to gather more facts.

This quickly resulted in conflicts between early scientists and Christianity, which had claimed that divine guidance had given it understanding of the universe. Galileo's observations about the orbit of the Earth conflicted with the pronouncements of the Catholic pope. Centuries later, Darwin's theory of evolution challenged the Bible, a theory that still remains a source of division.

As science enabled rationality to become ever more impressive, rationality became the public language, and one that everybody could agree on. This came in very handy, as the extreme corruption at the top of the Catholic Church had caused fractures in that Church. Protestants, who left the Church in rebellion against this corruption, and Catholics, who remained, needed common ground. Secularist, rationalist ideas provided this common ground and quickly spread. Those ideas that were argued for on this basis of guidance became a matter for the private sphere, and public life became dominated by what could be argued for based on commonly accepted observations and assumptions, with basic tenets of morality admitted as assumptions in intellectual systems of rationality.

Science and rationality have had such highly visible and world-changing successes that, by now, some of us expect science to have explained nearly everything. The people of Newton's time experienced 'experimental philosophy', later known as science, suddenly providing a clear understanding of a subject they'd long discussed, the movement of heavenly bodies. Duly impressed, they decided to do more experiments. After a few short centuries of rapid increases in scientific knowledge, many of us don't want to discuss things not proven by science. Science has acquired a semi-religious status for some people, who have faith that science is, or will soon be, a guide to all of life's questions. In the 20th century, this notion acquired the derogatory name 'scientism' (originally due to Hayek[30]). It has been challenged by failures of science to answer many questions, as well as scientific results that question the possibility of perfect knowledge. However, like other deep attachments, it has tended to bend rather than break.

The arc of scientific discovery shows that the scientific method is not equally able to answer all questions. In particular, the social sciences have struck many people as much less precise than physics – to put it mildly. As noted in the section on definitions, as we move away from thinking about particles, to larger and larger wholes, we often tend to think less and less precisely. There are some rules and principles in subjects like economics and neuroscience, but they do not typically lead to airtight understanding. A large degree of intuition and judgement is required to use what knowledge science provides wisely, constructing an inevitably imperfect, but useful, understanding of society.[31]

The level of remaining faith in science is highly variable in society. Scientists and the educated elites who are most influenced by scientific culture are often accused of paying 'lip service' to the idea of our limited reason. We will return to this in the discussion of rationality.

I will end this section by calling attention to how far the status of guidance has fallen, since the rise of science. Monkhood, a life devoted to cultivating guidance, was considered the most noble of professions. Today, someone announcing a choice of monastic life is often met with concern or condescension. This is reflected in the endangerment of monastic or contemplative life generally. Moving to more extreme choices, a saint who lives in a forest is now considered something akin to a madman by most Westerners.

Buddhism

Note: some readers familiar with Buddhism may understandably be tempted to skip parts of this section. Even if you skip parts, you are invited to read the section on true insight.

Introduction

No term like 'Buddhism' actually exists in traditionally Buddhist cultures. Instead it is called something like 'the Way of Awakening'. Rather than giving intellectual truths, most Buddhist schools see themselves as communities whose main purpose is the transmission of ways to see truth. A Buddha is a person who is considered to have awakened to (opened her or his eyes to) the most important truths, which cannot be either taught or said directly. Siddhartha Gautama, known as 'the Buddha', is just the most famous of many such people who founded a particularly effective tradition of teaching. I've encountered this tradition primarily through Plum Village, the community of the Zen Master Thich Nhat Hanh, but it is a vast tradition that I will sketch in very brief detail.

Westerners are paying increasing attention to the Buddhist 'Way of Awakening' because it has stood the test of 2,600 years of time, and has stark differences from the Christian tradition that was undercut by science, and because Western science has come to agree with many of its claims. Like science, Buddhist tradition holds that knowledge should be actively generated and confirmed by observation. It also holds, though, that observing phenomena in our own consciousness clearly is very hard, so the insights discussed below are not widely understood. Instead, our view of our own mind is blurred by constant thoughts that we mistake for ourselves. Most of us will know what is meant by the phrase 'I don't have time to hear myself think.' Meditation involves hearing yourself think very deeply.

A few specific events that have contributed to Buddhism's growing reputation within scientific circles are: 1) the teaching common across traditions that mindfulness practice can alleviate has been tested by scientific investigation and found considerable support;[32] 2) its long-standing claims that the reality we commonly experience is constructed or created, and also inspired by an actuality larger than ourselves, agrees with Western philosophy of recent centuries and with contemporary neuroscience;[33,34] 3) its observations on the artificiality of the self concept have been echoed by thinkers reflecting on the findings of neuroscience;[35] and 4) its insistence on the unity and inseparability of all things is consistent with our current understanding of physics.[36] It seems unlikely that Buddhism could have anticipated these conclusions of science if its ways of understanding were not worthwhile. So, we might want to seriously consider some of its other central contentions, not yet tested by science.

What has prevented Buddhism being taken more seriously?

I will start this section by discussing the factors that have made it difficult for the West to consider the Buddhist teachings more seriously, up until now.

The first factor is that Buddhism is considered 'a religion' and therefore, like Christianity, it is typically considered to be 'unscientific'. Buddhism, to the Western mind, is what some people have instead of Christianity, even though its actual beliefs have been noted to be quite different. What makes Buddhism different from Christianity, and other Abrahamic religions, is its claims about the sources of its teachings. Though the inner experiences of long-dead people are the *original* source of teachings, the tradition also teaches that it can be tested by any suitably disciplined, undistracted person, who can concentrate and calm their mind enough to observe closely and to think clearly. In fact, only such people really understand what the Way of Awakening teaches. Buddhists say many (at least thousands) have done this, and found little to disagree with. Of course, many who identify as Buddhists have not really looked into the matter seriously themselves, relying on the authority of those 'spiritual masters'.

Another common reason for dismissing Buddhism is that the belief in many lives (reincarnation) has been common in some Buddhist cultures, which is taken to prove that the tradition is a superstitious attempt to deny mortality, as Christianity is accused of being. Firstly, not all Buddhists believe in something akin to reincarnation and it was never taught by Gautama as an integral part of his teachings.[37] The Buddha himself never claimed to know for certain that there is reincarnation because of his disciplined direct observations of consciousness – the method that anticipated many contemporary scientific conclusions several thousand years ago. Instead, the belief in many lives was common among the wisest people of his culture, and he saw nothing to directly contradict it. In other words, if Gautama believed in reincarnation, this was likely because it was the received expert opinion of his time, not because he felt that it was revealed through his own enquiry. Though all schools of Buddhism hold that insights discussed below are best understood through direct observation of consciousness, I know of no Buddhist school that claims the truth of reincarnation can be directly observed. A number (including Zen, the tradition I focus on) have de-emphasised or rejected the notion of many lives.[38] Many practitioners see it as incompatible with the core belief in the impermanence of all things and the insight of no-self.

Another reason why Buddhism has not been taken seriously in the West is the tendency to take one's culture's own ideas more seriously than those of others, which hardly needs explanation. Philosophers who are routinely cited at length in Western literature, believed in things at least as ridiculous as reincarnation but are not dismissed. Aristotle believed, for example, that there are some people who are born to be slaves, and the function of the brain is to cool the blood.[39] But no one suggests we dismiss all his other ideas, showing that different standards are being applied to Eastern traditions of enquiry than to Western ones.

The teaching of Nirvana is also a reason why Buddhism has not been taken more seriously. This quality of mind, like Buddhism's version of heaven, is known only by the claims of a few prophets. Buddhists hold that the ability to dwell in Nirvana is rare, but that hundreds are thought to have entered into it, and many thousands of living beings have experienced related states of Kensho or Satori, which are states of non-conceptual (non-dual) awareness in which the nature of the mind is seen clearly, but which are still not Nirvana.

Another reason that Buddhism has not been taken seriously is that it is misunderstood by being seen as a philosophy. Well-meaning people suggest this as an alternative to the idea that Buddhism is a religion, but this simply invites an understanding of Buddhism through another poor analogy. Western philosophy builds systems of thoughts that are consistent with one another and with what can easily be observed. Buddhist tradition, however, counsels *expanding what can be observed*, by practising disciplined looking at the mind's inner workings. It also holds that its core insights cannot be understood, affirmed or denied by those who have not managed to be able to observe their own mind with great inner stillness. Even then, they are deeply in touch with their own nature at a level outside of words. In this way, the mind is sometimes likened to a pond that is calm enough to reflect what is going on around it. Thought creates ripples on the surface. The picture of a philosopher pondering a problem such as Rodin's *Thinker*, or that of a Buddha, illustrates this difference more clearly than words can.

Figure 2 Rodin's Thinker and the Buddha of Kamakura represent embodied ideals of Western philosophical and Buddhist traditions – the differences are all-important to Buddhism
(source: Rodin's Thinker – Andrew Horne ; Buddha of Kamakura – Miriam Thyes)

Buddhism has some teachings that are useful to express and understand intellectually, which guide its practitioners and which, it holds, can survive intellectual questioning. But it also has practices, such as meditation, which could be described as 'mystical' – for example, the intellect plays only a small role in mindfulness meditation, which involves looking at the world without any preconceptions – as we would something totally mysterious. Nowadays, mindfulness is taught in hospitals, schools, prisons and elsewhere, often using public funds. Paradoxically, then, the most seemingly mystical part of Buddhism is now widespread, while the parts that invite the label of 'philosophy' are less understood. This is actually not such a bad development from a Buddhist perspective, because mindfulness meditation is a traditional way to achieve the deeper understandings that Buddhist concepts point towards. Still, though, it is important to note that mindfulness has traditionally been taught as just one important part of an approach to life.

Mindfulness

The word 'mindfulness' is traditionally used to refer to a basic 'quality of mind' that arises along with an unjudging presence or 'being, here, now'. Just as there are basic primary sets of colours that can be experienced visually, on the level of inner experience there are various kinds of 'feeling tones' in our conscious experience, and one of these is associated with the word mindfulness. Academic philosophers and scientists might call this feeling a kind of 'qualia', while some spiritual people, including Thich Nhat Hanh, call it a kind of 'energy'.[40] I prefer to call it a 'quality of mind'.

The quality of mindfulness is most intensely felt in those moments when our attention is totally devoted to *and* receptive to what is happening, right now – institutionalised mindfulness rhetoric uses terms like 'observing with non-judgemental awareness' to describe this. While we are aware of life in this way, the world seems to slow down. We might perceive a bird's wings flapping incredibly slowly, or we might be absorbed for a while with the pleasing slow motion of families of rustling leaves. After hearing this description, people often say, 'but I don't need a mindfulness practice – my mind has this quality while I'm fishing (or gardening, walking in nature, etc.).' They know, rightly, that we all experience profound mindfulness at times. It is not a state invented by meditators; mindfulness practice is meant to be cultivation of this naturally occurring phenomenon.

The radical contention, however, of 'the Way of Awakening' (a more direct translation of what Buddhism is actually called in the East), is that we can be deeply mindful very often, and that this way of being leads to less suffering. The point of mindfulness practice is not only to be mindful while gardening, but while in a traffic jam on a hot summer day with an argument going on next to you. If we do this, we can see deeply into the nature of suffering. This, however, is hard.

The word 'mindfulness' that Buddhists use, to gesture towards this quality of non-judgemental awareness, has become associated with a popularising movement that is increasingly profit driven, so some find that the word *mindfulness* feels 'icky', to use a non-technical term. Mindfulness may now be associated, for many of us, with a mentality of achievement and productivity, a mechanism for coping with ugly, sterile or dog-eat-dog environments, but mindfulness practice is an age-old element of Buddhism. Traditionally, people who wanted to become really good at being mindful often chose to change their jobs. Mindfulness meditation helps to calm the mind, and anything that helps will be monetised in our culture. The problem is not mindfulness, but a commercial culture that will make an attractive commodity out of anything useful, distorting such things in the process.[41]

Mindfulness is not a procedure, or even a technique, that we can simply hand over to people, though there are techniques that we can use to create conditions in which mindfulness most easily emerges. Following the breath is the most famous of those, but there are more useful techniques than can be named. Mindfulness, as mentioned, comes most easily when one is not focused on, and is giving great importance to, words and thoughts. So sitting still and following our own breath gives us a pretty good chance to be mindful because we don't have ingrained habits of thinking while in this state. Our breath is deeply connected to everything that goes on in our body, so following it gives us a chance to notice the little pulses of emotion that herald the arrival of a judgey thought. Using this technique is an art; the part of the mind that is not technical is very important in mindfulness.

Attachment

Attachment is very closely related to desire: it occurs when we mentally grasp onto an outcome or an idea. We all get attached to things, whether sex or drugs, or spending time with our friends. Taking things for granted and becoming attached to them go hand in hand – when we take something for granted, we expect it so strongly that we hardly notice any pleasure when we get it, but we experience pain when we lose it.

Attachment comes with *heavy* expectations, and they drive all manner of emotions. When we do not have what we are attached to, but think that we can achieve it, we are excited and driven. When we expect something but do not get it, we get annoyed, frustrated or angry. When we are attached to something but lose it, we become sad. When we are not attached, we are just calm in the face of change. Being 'unattached' does not mean we have no expectations – it means that we are ready to let go of them.

This description is conceptual, however, and might not resonate with some readers. To help, I'll share the following personal stories:

Long ago, when I was at a Boy Scout summer camp, we were making our way through a pack of candy that a few of us had pooled our money to buy ('Nerds', I think), when we noticed that there was a mail-in prize competition advertised on the packet. Thousands of dollars of prizes were there to be won, and to us, it was life-changing amounts of money. We mused about the possibilities of the prizes at stake, and in our unrestricted childish imaginations the musings quickly acquired lifelike resolution, and we were nearly living the new lives that Nerds were offering.

Then, suddenly, when our conversation had driven us to some new height of titillation, the question of sharing arose. Details are hazy, but it went something like this: my friend Steve and I had split the cost of the pack of Nerds, and were planning on sharing the prize. Somebody else pointed out that he had shared much better candy that he'd brought from home freely, and thought that this should entitle him to a share of the prize. Others thought that we should just split the prize equally, for their various reasons. Ideas differed. I clearly remember the instant when eyes shifted around our loose circle and souls coiled as us kids looked for a chance to make up winning sides in the argument. At some point, it occurred to me that this was all over some prizes that were a lot like the lottery tickets that my aunt and mother usually bought and threw away with sighs that were small, and even then seemed half-feigned.

I blurted this out. We all realised immediately that we were being stupid, and passions waned, we exchanged the sorts of apologies that our mothers had made us rehearse over the years, and we returned to being friends and went swimming. I think we threw out the prize mail-in form, in an act of solidarity. I think even then I regarded this as a life lesson. It was one of those occasions where you watch your mind run away from reality. Looking back, I would say that the lesson we learned was one in attachment.

It is uncontroversially unwise to attach yourself to lottery prizes. Adults play their own lottery with individual tickets, but generally, they do not care much when they lose. It seems to me that people are more attached to the small thrill that comes from the possibility of winning – this is a regular and reliable element of the experience, the ritualistic part that you can hold on to, without getting burned. It's a bit like how, when the ability to experience sexual desire is a new thing, we get infatuated with celebrities but learn to just enjoy looking at them and vicariously experiencing their life. We are all intuitive experts in attachment, and while the common wisdom is to get attached, it is to get attached to things that have a level of certainty or that are worth the risk. The uncommon wisdom of the Buddha is that since nothing is sure, there is only certainty of cessation, and so nothing is worth the risk: better to simply not be attached to anything. It is possible to live this way, though this requires total concentration. And living this way is joyful.

I found out that nothing is a sure thing, nothing is forever, at a young age. When I was in the second grade my father had a seizure while driving on a late November day and lost control of his vehicle. His truck swerved into a lake and he drowned. He worked two jobs, running a construction company, and teaching calculus in high school, and was not around too much, but when he was, he was a character. He was big and tall and garrulous and charismatic, and people loved him. A tough guy who was full of laughs and stories around the dinner table. He was smart and fierce; he also used to coach American football, leading his school to state dominance in eight years as coach before retiring to try his hand at construction. He walked like a guy who did that, and my little chest swelled with pride being around him. I felt tough too. He was also sensitive, lying on the bed face down and crying when the family dog died. We really hung onto those legs tight when he was around, literally attaching ourselves to him with as tight a grip as our young bodies could muster.

They had his funeral in the gymnasium of St Lawrence High School and people filed past the casket in lines, and told us how sorry they were. I still remember the persistent shocks at realising, time and again, that he wasn't coming home tonight, again. In the early evening according to schedule, anticipation of his presence arose. It was impossible to let go of the sensations that felt so real. The anticipation of the routine that had been so solid for so long is deep and unconscious and lawlike, and it is only at certain points in life – when suddenly it is yanked away – that you find out how deep it is. We foolishly made our mother and aunt promise to us that they wouldn't die too. It was impossible to entertain the idea that something similar could happen again. Taking the view that God couldn't possibly let this happen to us twice helped to chase this away; it helped reliably – I found myself quite attached to that one. But it was obviously untrue, and so we needed it to feel more real, and hearing things make them seem real, so we were in turn attached to asking again and again for confirmation that Mommy and Auntie would not go and die, and hearing 'no' in a certain voice.

We grasp onto reliable things, the big and safe embrace of a parent, our soft bed and drink in the evening. They make their impressions into our memories, and we turn memories into anticipations, and anticipations beget cravings. Just look at your life, and you will see this directly. Cravings are fulfilled and strengthened over and over again, and over and over, establishing ever more well-worn, deep impressions of experience in our inner life, the habits of 'feeling real' about things that make up reality. 'Reifying' and attaching are the same thing. If all goes well, these things don't one day vanish suddenly and leave us with our drives, our cravings calling out to be met in vain. We cannot avoid awareness that this is possible, so attachment will always be met with existential dread of the fringe of consciousness. That is why unattachment has been seen as the route to joy and freedom.

Action through inaction

Buddhism is distinguished from the Western mainstream in its emphasis on implicit (non-verbal) knowledge and its ability to guide our actions. Guidance is the natural state that we find ourselves in when we can stop grasping at thoughts and plans, but it is not a focus of Western life. That is why some Westerners think Buddhism is about sitting still. I will use sports to illustrate the distinction between behaviours that 'flow from awareness' and those that are 'decided upon', which I hope will show that guidance is not otherworldly.

When we watch a sport, we often hear the commentators talk about the 'good decisions' that a player makes, but we know from experience that when we actually play a sport, we often don't experience ourselves making decisions at all. Instead, things seem to happen automatically or 'in the flow', especially when we are playing well.[42] However, from the standpoint of a commentator, the things she sees players doing can be *discussed as though* they result from decisions. This is because this way of seeing things helps us to see alternatives that a player or a team could be pursuing instead. Their coach may look at things this way to try to nudge them towards these decisions. The fans look at things this way to have fun second-guessing the players, and to get excited about what might have been.

At the same time, talking about athletes' actions as decisions introduces confusion, because conscious decisions involve, first, considering a number of alternatives, and second, taking actions that are consistent with one alternative. In sports, we often don't have time for all that – we just have to make a play. Commentators have time to consciously imagine a number of alternative plays that a player could have made. They are using their ability to experience space and time to imagine a number of things the players could have done at a point in time, while the players are *being* in space and time, dealing with the practicalities of playing a game as time carries them forward.

Players who, according to commentators, 'make good decisions' in basketball or football are also said to 'see the court (or field) well'. Actually, what lies underneath the good decisions is the players' awareness, to a greater or lesser extent, of the flow and happenings of the game. This awareness translates to a more sensitive and immersed experience in which the game seems to happen more slowly: a ball may even seem larger, and players make plays that contribute to a win.

Sports give us wonderful situations in which to understand the benefits of acting through awareness, because they are designed in ways that encourage players to constantly be attentive. If we play sports in a way that is mechanical, we lose, so we learn to 'be there'. The pace is often too fast to allow deliberation. Sports are thus a place where many of us experience being in flow, though the flow that we experience in sports can be experienced in all avenues of life. In other parts of life, the distinction between conscious deliberation and acting in the flow is less stark. Deliberation works better in an office than it does in sports, and it works to help us make moral decisions. Yet deliberation and flow in moral life and sporting life are related. Deliberation is made out of words, and it is easy and natural to talk about; flow, like love, is not easy to talk about (see section on equality for more). These experiences don't give themselves over to intellectual understanding but they are all important for finding our path.

Nirvana

I cannot explain Nirvana to you, but I hope to get you to consider that it is not as silly a thing as it can seem, and that trying to understand it *is* silly.

Nirvana, as mentioned, has been thought of as 'Buddhist heaven', but really, it is said to be what arises when one *totally extinguishes attachments, including to concepts*. The ability to totally let go of attachments is rare – and that is what earns a person the title 'Buddha' – but many practitioners feel they get something like a fleeting glimpse of Nirvana's clarity and joy. Buddhist teachers approach Nirvana differently from how Christian priests approach heaven, typically speaking little about Nirvana, given its prominence in perceptions of Buddhism. I won't try to explain Nirvana clearly to you, either – not even the few people who are said to dwell in it can – but I'll try to communicate my humble understanding of why it might be so elusive, even if it is actually possible.

It would make sense to me that Nirvana is impossible to clearly describe to anybody who has never completely let go of all attachments, even if Nirvana is a real thing. Many things need to be seen, directly, to be really understood. If Nirvana were real, speaking about it to a person with no direct insight into it could only create, in that listener's mind, a sort of metaphor that draws on something the listener has experienced. The experience of describing colour to the colour blind is one example.[43] The same is true of speaking about skydiving to a non-skydiver – we get them to imagine something based on their past experience. But that person just has to jump out of a plane with a parachute to find out for themselves what skydiving is like. In contrast, a person would have to let go of any conceptual expectations about Nirvana that the description of Nirvana created in order to enter into Nirvana itself. So maybe it is understandable why not much is said about it, and why few people actually enter into it.

However, we all know the joy of being quite content with what is, of not having many thoughts in mind, but being immersed in the beauty of now. So maybe we can relate to Nirvana through this more common, but still rare, experience. We can see there is something interesting about not being caught up in concepts, but it's best not to dwell on imagining what this is like, because then we are creating an expectation. It seems more useful to relate to the elusiveness of Nirvana through the elusiveness of beauty. If you go outside and pick the nearest cloud out of the sky, and try to see the beauty in this cloud as deeply as you've ever seen the beauty in any cloud that you've ever seen, you'd probably fail very badly. You will be occupied with finding your expectation of beauty in the image of the cloud, not with just letting the cloud fill up your awareness, which is what happens on the way to experiences of beauty. Failing to let go of attachments is like that, which might be the most profound thing I can say about Nirvana based on my own experience.

Even if meditators *believe* attachment is unwise, our minds, like others, tend to acquire attachments to things that are very pleasing, and the idea of Nirvana is pleasing. More mundane kinds of happiness, like contentment and beauty, are also impaired by our attachment to them. This can be frustrating, but rather than just giving up on cultivating our appreciation of these, Buddhism suggests being fully aware of and accepting our attachments, and that this place of awareness is the best place from which to release these attachments.

True insight vs intellectual insight

Western society does not dwell enough on the distance between merely believing a statement and deeply seeing the truth of it. This is the same as knowing something at a merely intellectual level, versus having true insight (also known as heart understanding, embodied understanding, direct knowing and so on). Our emphasis on the intellect obscures the importance of alignment between intellect and the rest of mind, so necessary for integrity.

For example, most of us agree with *the idea* that we cause suffering by not listening to people. We can still ignore people constantly, though, while avoiding actual awareness of the pain we cause – after all, our attention is on something else while they are trying to be heard. We don't see their faces fall, don't notice their eyes looking at ours, looking for some acknowledgement of what they are saying; maybe we notice some frustration or dejection. Personally, when I am merely intellectually aware that not listening is hurtful, I still ignore people, but while having guilt in the back of my mind.

Being fully aware of the self-superiority or selfishness that lies behind this behaviour is more difficult than verbally admitting I have these traits. Transforming into a good listener gets us into 'spiritual' territory. It involves allowing our experience of the way we feel when we are ignored to become awareness of the way others must feel when they are ignored.

Conviction is what our minds have worked into our bones and what our bones have worked into our minds. It follows from the depth to which we see into something – whether it is another person's pain, the value of a project or anything else. We cannot completely avoid awareness of this distinction in life – we all note the difference between a person who abstractly supports a particular ideal (lying is almost always unwise) and one who will go to great lengths to be in line with it (does not, for example, misrepresent his opinion of a friend's work).

When it wouldn't even occur to us to lie, we have total conviction about honesty. When we simply agree that lying is bad but continue doing it, then we do not. There is, of course, a lot of space in between. Where we are in that space depends on how aware we have become of the impacts our past lies have had, on the stress and dissonance of maintaining two versions of the truth, and so on.

Our knowledge of our own inevitable death is another example of knowledge that can stay at the intellectual level. When one stills the mind in meditation, there is seldom total quiet, but rather stubborn thoughts and feelings cling to the fringe of awareness, moving in the shadows. Some of the most disturbing of these have to do with dying, because one is attached to what is called 'I' and would like to imagine and anticipate that it will remain present. Of course, we know at another level that it is impermanent, but have grasped onto the thing called I, and almost none of us let go of it no matter how plain the evidence is that we are going to end, just like everybody else. The more we release attachment to life continuing, though, and accept uncertainty and impermanence, the more death can come out of the shadows. The more beliefs such as impermanence turn into convictions, the less tension there is between our ideas and actuality.

Aligning convictions with our rational beliefs and our perceptions is much harder than changing our beliefs. This is the sort of thing, though, that makes us wiser. We can look at the spiritual path as learning to question what we think we know, and to question our feelings, and then bringing thoughts and feelings into concert, so that we know basic truths in our bones and minds and act in accordance with them. Then we are well guided.

3 Major Attachments
and Their Shadows

I F WE find ourselves experiencing a great deal of suffering then, as Zen teaches, our greatest attachments are the first place to look for a remedy. *Rationality*, *individuality* and *equality* are central views that Western culture has become attached to, and so they can cause great suffering. Attachments are eventually a source of suffering, because nothing is permanent and no concept is totally true. This is an idea that we see repeated in science, where a long history of discarding ideas has forced us to accept that theories are never correct, just less wrong. As also mentioned, though, our understanding of our beliefs' imperfections tends to be 'merely intellectual' – when ideas work well, then we get deeply attached to them and treat them as true.[44] Abstractly, belief in our ideas' limitations is a good start, but it matters about as much in terms of our ability to use ideas humbly as believing that exercise is good helps us to work out daily.

Certain ideas – that we can rationally understand the world, and that we are independent individuals with 'our own lives' that we are in control of, and that we are all 'equal' – have served us well, and in the process, have become *the truth*.

These three attachments, however, are not, like scientific ideas, just about the way things *are* but also moral ideas about how things should be. Attachment to them distorts the way the world occurs to us, how we see ourselves and what about ourselves we can see. For example, deep belief in the power of rationality implies that problems can be solved, that people who are rational will be effective, and that fuzzy intuitions that are out of line are not as important as logic. This ideal, and a widespread attachment to being good, means that many tend to see themselves as rational, and suppress feelings that cannot be justified. Those who do not internalise the superiority of rationality, and who instead speak from guidance have also tended to be pushed to the fringes of social awareness just as the awareness of death is pushed to the fringe of personal awareness. Of course, this marginalisation has decreased in recent years, but I hope to convince readers what a long way there is still left to go.

It is worth pointing out that these legacies of Western Enlightenment thought are not the only ideas that are commonly held with a near dogmatic tightness. Another core belief that has been shown to create ghastly shadows is the idea that we are 'civilised' in relation to other humans (which has justified unspeakable colonial treatment of 'the uncivilised'). Interwoven with that is the idea that we are separate from or above nature, which as Joanna Macy and others have pointed out, underlies our move towards environmental catastrophe, keeping us from seeing how we belong to and depend on nature. I discuss the current triad because they are relatively recent additions to our core beliefs, very different from other cultures, which determine our worldview and shadows. They are the outer layer of the ideological onion of the West, as it were.

It is also worth noting that I do not claim to have invented the notion that this triad of attachments is uniquely important for the West or that they can be problematic. For example, the loss of faith in rationality-driven progress is a core element of postmodernism and is well-represented in radical environmentalism.[45] The point of this short book is to discuss why these attachments remain, and how they are contributing to societal trends which seem surreal and dangerous, and to suggest alternative approaches using an approach informed by Zen Buddhism. I would direct readers to Richard Tarnas's fine book *The Passion of the Western Mind* for a thorough and satisfying intellectual history of all these ideas, and to Larry Siedentop's *Inventing the Individual* for a history of the individual, particularly. I discuss their history relatively little, quite intentionally. I prefer to appeal to our direct experience of these ideas, which really need no introduction, and how they align, or do not, with the world they are supposed to describe.

Rationality

The way in which we became attached to rationality has already been discussed, because it is so central to the background of our world; I couldn't have got this far without writing about it. What is more important to discuss now, after discussing Zen, is its emotional weight, because this is what really underlies our faith in rationality – something our rationalist worldview itself prevents us from seeing. Achieving consistency between beliefs by updating them is important for rationality, but our emotional attachment to answers is what prevents us from being able to question them. Our attachment to the idea that rationality can give us the answers we need is driven by how great it feels when rationality works.

The attachment to rationality

It is good to get in touch with our deeper feelings about rationality by asking: 'what has intellect and rationality ever done for us?'

Let's look around. As I write this section, I have an almost perfectly flat floor to rest my feet on that is about six metres above the ground, and I am typing on an eerily sleek-looking machine that creates letters on a page, shows video images of an inexhaustible number of hours, and can have food delivered to my door. It does this by making precise logical computations at mind-boggling speeds. Our ancestors would take one look at it and have been certain that magic was at work. And they would scarcely believe that the objects that travel through the sky above me, without flapping their wings, are carrying people – often, within a few hours, to lands that our ancestors didn't know about.

I could go on for pages. To see how much we value knowledge, note that inventors and scientists like Thomas Edison are 'immortal' – their names live on more surely than billionaires'. When we want to make a cutting insult, we call people stupid, morons, idiots, all words for low intelligence. Those who show too much intelligence are often resented, because they make others feel bad about themselves. Nobody is resented for having too much of something that is unimportant.

We probably don't even really realise how deeply we value rational explanations because actually it is somewhat taboo to talk directly about intelligence (which our culture defines as the ability to explain things). The difficulty and resistance that we feel in relation to talking about something is always in proportion to its emotional weight.

I hope this puts you in touch with the kinds of *feelings* we have towards intellect and its products in our culture. Still, like a parent that has been there for us, we don't actually have any idea how attached we are to all of the miracles that science and reason have brought to us, hundreds of years after their first rise. Attachment to behaviours and things often comes when they can be so 'taken for granted' as to become invisible.

The Western cultural notion that it experienced 'an enlightenment' and has since been 'progressing' is held in place (or reified) by tangible pleasures that reason has put at our fingertips. This is why it is so important to remember that chart of income and well-being I reprinted in Figure 1: for a long time, as we became 'more rational' and advanced technically, and incomes went up, life became easier, safer and more pleasurable; collectively, we have inherited our attitudes and feelings about rationality from that time. But our innovation has changed our context, and, as mentioned at the beginning, letting go of ideas that stop being useful when context changes is a big part of wisdom.

Certainty and control

But what does it mean to be addicted to rationality? Rationality is deeply connected to conceptual knowledge; it involves finding concepts that can predict the world and allow us to control it. Concepts are about generalisations, as mentioned above: when we find rules, we can make things happen.

Addictions ultimately are to sensations – the good feelings we get from something, whether that thing is cocaine, pizza, orgasm or a scientific discovery. The pleasurable sensations that we get from rationality are feelings of stimulation and wonder, and also of certainty and control. The former arise when we engage with something we don't understand, and the latter when we look at the world and see consistency with what we already know – when our projections of expectations onto the world match what we see. This means we feel good. When we know that we can get what we want, that is even better. We are used to getting these good feelings a lot.

We have built a world within which things work as they are supposed to. Running water is one example. Computer screens are another. Compare making letters by pressing keys with writing by hand. Wow! The newer method, arrived at through technology, is highly reliable. You might object and say that you get annoyed with technology all the time. However, this can't be true, because annoyance comes when expectations are not met. We get especially annoyed that computers don't work *and we remember these incidents* because we have so many forgettable, predictable interactions with tech.

It is interesting to contrast typing with more chaotic activities, like cooking. When cooking, we get used to things not going like they are supposed to. The beans start to soften in four hours instead of two. Good cooks look and taste inquisitively and are ready to adjust: they expect the unexpected. Cooking tends to put us into a leisurely mindset, inquisitive and present. We often just trust our instincts. Compare that with computers: we get annoyed with the smallest delay in opening a web page because computers are normally very easy to control.

There is a basic feeling of being certain, and in control, when everything goes according to plan, and we are on automatic – and these are pleasurable feelings. Internally consistent, logically consistent frameworks feel good and so does watching a computer do exactly what we make it do. We are just so used to these sensations that we don't feel them any more, just as we often don't taste breakfast cereal. But we discover how attached we are to things working when they break – when the computer freezes or when a waiter doesn't do what we want, or when our cereal runs out.

Rationality and climate change

It could be objected, in response to what I've written, that actually, we are not rational enough. We've ignored science the whole way to our present climate crisis. But why have we done this? Partly because we have too much faith in rationality and its famed products – technology, science and profit-driven business, and partly because we overestimate the degree to which we are actually rational.

Consider the common objection that calls for climate activism are overblown because we don't know for certain whether climate change will become dangerous in a few decades, or in 50 to 100 years. At the base of this excuse for doing nothing is *scientism*, the belief that science can answer all questions precisely. Scientism is an ideology fuelled by an attachment to the certainty and control we feel when we pace around on the island of order we've managed to dam off from the waters of chaos: houses and computers and cars, where things function like they're supposed to almost all the time.

If we can do it in time, we *should* understand climate change perfectly before acting. But unfortunately, climate science is the type of science that doesn't give us that feeling of certainty and control, because it studies something that is well beyond the level of particles, highly complex and beyond our abilities to experimentally test. In scientific experiments, we can isolate and control one member of a certain kind of entity (e.g. a pure form of a particular substance, like carbon), and through manipulations we can find rules that apply to similar kinds of entities out there in the world. Then we can predict those entities and act to influence them precisely. Though climate science may use physics, it does not seek to describe the results inside the artificial conditions of laboratories. It describes a large system that we have no copies of – the Earth. This system is beyond our means to fully measure and it is fantastically complex.

We are running experiments on this system, building a prototype you might say, with our carbon emissions, but hard experimental results that will tell us what happens to the Earth when it warms by 2°C will come when the planet itself reaches 2°C higher. The idea that we will get a perfect model before this experiment is run is a fantasy of scientism. Science needs experiments to be sure, so we will never be completely sure that climate science is accurate until it is too late.

It might be helpful to entertain the following analogy. The Earth is often likened to a single organism. So, our situation is a bit like finding an exotic animal from the Amazon, one that we will never replace, which is not quite like any other animal that we know of. We know the animal stays healthy under certain conditions – the ones it has always existed in. We then run experiments on it, measure its internal processes by taking measurements and scraping a few pieces off the organism, and then look at some of them under the microscope. The results of our experiments, combined with our understanding of basic science, lead us to suspect that the organism will react badly if we change its conditions, but we run an experiment anyway, because we aren't *sure*. We see signs that the life form is not responding very well to what we are doing, but because we don't know yet *for sure* that it will get very ill, we decide not to panic, and continue with the experiment.

This may sound insane, because it is, obviously. If we wanted to preserve the life form in a healthy state, we would stop the experiments fast. This is a pretty simple and relatively accurate analogy, but we don't see our experiments on the Earth in the same light because of one detail I've omitted – the scientists' experiment (in reality, carbon emissions) is pleasurable to them (humans). We could imagine the scientists finding that the fragments of the creature have extraordinary narcotic effects. It's as though we've decided that because we would *really like* to know just how much we can extract from this organism before it collapses, we can know. This leap of faith is enabled by centuries of scientism. The same ideology might allow our addicted scientists to remain confident in their ability to heal the rare creature after it is deeply damaged (bio-engineering).

This is not necessarily enabled by science itself, which *can be* conscious of its limits – ironically scientists themselves are quite cognisant of science's limits. Rather, this is about a general cultural attitude pervading society, a faith that science and technology will save the day – or that science can and should provide us with certainty (before we act). But this expectation – even an obsession – for this kind of knowledge is dysfunctional. Perfect scientific knowledge is great but often not feasible. Sometimes, you have to look at the big picture, and the facts available, sense the trade-offs and the inevitable ignorance, and act based on judgement, which is frighteningly 'subjective'. We will eventually have to trust our sense of guidance and make a decision.

Another example of rationality gone wrong is the kind of statement that goes, 'yes, those climate scientists say that we're heading towards disaster, but if they are right, why isn't everybody else scared?' For example, news articles sometimes focus on the opinions of Warren Buffet and Bill Gates, who are optimistic, which seem to offer reassurance.[46,47] Underlying such sentiments, I think, is faith that society as a whole, or at least smart leaders in business and technology, must understand our situation and be able to deal with it (we are collectively rational).

Now stop and ask yourself: why on earth do individuals tend to take the word of Buffet and Gates or society at large, over the small army of highly intelligent people who spend all of their time working on climate science? The reason Buffet and Gates are optimistic is because they have a general faith in the intelligence of markets and the cleverness of technology, just like everybody else. Not because either of them have a concrete, worked-out solution. This is unsurprising because one is an investor and the other a technologist, and markets and technology are at the centre of societal myths about rationality and progress. Wider faith in markets and technology is why these billionaires are put on the news as counterpoints to climate scientists, and this faith invested in them by the public feeds their private faith. My point isn't to make personal attacks on them; they didn't really ask to be put on pedestals in this way. I question the faith we place in the rationality of markets and the ability of science to create technology, which acts as a megaphone, amplifying every word of investors and technologists.

Depending on celebrity spokesmen for technology and markets is a way of dealing with the difficulty of going through the thorough, clear-headed and rigorous analysis of complicated and emotionally charged issues like climate change. The attraction of many to these men's utterances shows how difficult it is to be collectively rational. There is too much information to process and many opportunities to maintain unjustified optimism by latching onto the rare opinions of anybody who happens to be sceptical. It is easy to listen to first scientists, then sceptics, then Gates and Buffet, and then just shrug and conclude that you don't have time to get to the bottom of it, and that time will tell.

I've done this, and then realised my fellow voters are in the same boat. I then concluded that nothing will happen until there is a stark crisis that puts an end to all of the guesswork. Then I shrugged off that train of thought, and had it again a year later. This is where many people's efforts end up. Now with other kinds of crises mounting, we cannot replay the same sort of dynamic with our social issues. This is the time to have a conversation with our guts, question our core beliefs, and decide which ones to keep and which to revise, and to make a decision based on the subjective sense that emerges.

The idea that we are collectively rational, and therefore what we are doing *must be* rational, must be decisively discarded as a part of this process. I will now discuss Bill Gates' particular ideas about climate change both as a way of providing a concrete example of dangerous faith in technology, and as a way of transitioning to the next idea I see the need to let go of: individualism.

Bill Gates created the source of his vast fortune by marketing a computer operating system that unsophisticated users could use 30 years ago. He now spends money on technology to prevent climate change, but tellingly, not with the expectation of making money. He does this as a philanthropist, investing along with other Silicon Valley investors in 'energy miracles'. Having better technologies probably won't hurt, but in order to become widespread on a free market, these technologies will have to be better or less expensive than tech which is already there. But if there were a realistic possibility that technologists could quickly produce clean energy more cheaply than alternatives, on such a scale as to change our whole energy system, then philanthropy would be unnecessary. The market would be investing.

Technology cannot solve our problems alone, because we cannot by sheer force of will make it so that cleaner energy is cheaper than dirty energy. Dirty energy purveyors can innovate too, and ultimately technologies are in the world like Michelangelo's David was in the marble, waiting to be freed. There is a reason why again and again throughout history different people have invented exactly the same thing at almost the same time. Technologies are potentials that are discovered, not possibilities invented out of thin air. It is insane to bet our future on the hope that the cheapest potential source of vast amounts of energy, which is out there waiting to be found, will also just happen to be carbon free. It is especially insane to expect it to be so cheap that it will effortlessly displace *an energy infrastructure that is already built.*

But this hope is a large part of the reason for our climate inaction. It reveals a hubristic faith that it is possible to devise a clever *technical* solution for any bind we get into, if only we put our best people on it, and think long and hard enough. As you probably have gathered by now, I feel this is a belief that is there because it feels good, rather than because it makes sense. The truth is that our technological advances have already opened up many paths that are much better than the path we are pursuing. We just aren't pursuing them, because that would mean the collective making laws that affect choices of individuals. And collective action is impaired by individualism as discussed in the next chapter.

Before moving on, however, I will make the case that non-conceptual 'mysterious' insight should be accepted as something that is already part of life, and must be cultivated unashamedly if we are to finally gain the wisdom with which to guide our vast technological choices.

(Re)valuing mystery

The opposite of knowing it all is living contentedly with a sense of mystery and a lack of a need to explain it all. This does not mean sitting still. Explanations and analysis are useful parts of the human repertoire, but traditionally, it has been held that a certain amount of mystery is unavoidable, especially while engaging in great challenges. The word 'mysticism', which has the same root word as mystery, traditionally refers to the consultation of a kind of guidance available to us when we cease grasping at conceptual explanations. Mystical knowing is so fundamentally different from intellectual knowledge that it is sometimes called 'unknowing'. It does not come from thinking about the usefulness of various tactics and choices in an analytical manner but nevertheless it is capable of guiding our actions. When listening to our deepest source of intuition, we have the feeling of being guided, so I call this source *guidance*. This seems a useful term for disrupting our analytical culture's tendency to assume that only deliberative actions and plans can result in humans putting 'one foot in front of another' in a coherent way that allows us to survive.

Because of the many strange and awful things that have been justified by guidance, and because of the faith in rationality, the kind of knowledge that the mystical traditions cultivate is often filed under the topic of 'rainbows and unicorns'. The denial of its necessity is achieved by ignoring its presence in everyday life. Traditionally, and within non-scientific circles, this capacity for feeling our way through the mysterious is thought to be the source of artistic inspiration and taste, and a route to being deeply immersed in the beauty of existence. For example, when a person is in a situation where reason does not give a clear answer, there is often no better advice than 'looking deeply': sitting with a problem, waiting for words to come. Similarly, the ancient rite in many places across the world, of going to a mountaintop to sit in silence while fasting for several days, seems to elicit a similar mindset, and is commonly engaged in when a difficult and complex life choice is necessary. These are examples of concerted efforts to get deeply in touch with guidance, but this capacity for inexplicable intuitions plays a role in mundane life.

We have not fully investigated the power of guidance in responding to highly complicated social issues like climate change, because we have not been able to explain guidance in scientific terms, and thereby decisively re-legitimise it in the secular sphere.[48] Though psychology has studied this kind of ability for decades and documented its importance, it has not been able to reproduce the outcomes of guidance by precise analytical models of it. And yet this demand for analytical understanding is a demand by rationality to understand that which rationality is not capable of! But this demand remains influential because Western secular culture has internalised the idea that things that are real can be explained.

So, despite the much related research that has been done on what is here called guidance under the names of flow states,[49] implicit cognition,[50] intuition,[51] the Gestalt school of psychology,[52] emotional intelligence,[53] and type 3 processing,[54] secular conversations proceed almost as though analysis is the only way the mind navigates the world! Authors such as Heidegger and Nietzsche, psychiatrist Iain McGilchrist (who, joining others, associates guidance with the brain's right hemisphere), and many more, have all written persuasively that we are alienated from this same intelligence. Still, since science talks more about things because they are understood than because they are important, guidance is consistently de-emphasised in school curricula and public conversations.

So, it seems that the differences in the natures of analysis and of guidance mean that we have not been able to easily understand the character of one by using the other.

We might say guidance is a type of mental activity that is adapted for systems that are too large to be analytically tractable – to be described in a precise way in symbols and rules. Its contribution to us is our felt sense of direction, not our feeling of being able to grasp the precise meaning of things.

Contemplative mindsets can sound 'woo-woo' until we reflect on their acknowledged uses: musical composition is one, theoretical intuition is another, as is the impulse followed by thinkers who are sure of their direction but unable to explain it fully. We steadily use intuition the most while exploring difficult, open-ended questions with a vast range of possible answers, for example while arriving at, or building a theory to explain, mysterious evidence. These are exactly the kinds of choices that are difficult to assess in neatly controlled experiments. It may not be possible for the rational mind to feel as though it understands the dynamics underlying deep intuition. If the rational mind could understand the intuitive completely, then it could reproduce its results, and then there would be no need for the intuitive mind – and why would we have it in the first place? In this context, it is useful to remember the following phrases:

> If the mind were so simple that it could be understood,
> we would be so simple that we cannot understand it.

Emerson M. Pugh[55]

> Any sufficiently advanced technology is indistinguishable
> from magic

Arthur C. Clarke[56]

> Although we have to use reverse engineering to study the
> brain ... from our standpoint the brain is essentially a bit
> of alien technology

Patricia S. Churchland and Terrence J. Sejnowski[57]

All of these quotes point to the conclusion that it is only natural that the contents of our skulls and, relatedly, the nature of our minds, will remain indistinguishable from magic for some time. Personally, I think explanations such as divine inspiration can be ways of explaining away the magic, ways of grasping at certainty about where our guidance comes from and how much we can trust it. It is better to just listen to our guidance and let its exact nature remain mysterious; certainly the brain is involved, and probably the right hemisphere more than the left, but this tells us little except that natural selection put a lot of effort into crafting our guidance. A creature that is capable of understanding us as we are capable of understanding an amoeba might just be able to usefully explain our guidance. At this point in our history, we should just accept that it exists and use it.

The space that we must navigate to find our way to the best future still available to us now is one of great dimensions. Holding awareness of who we are as people, as a culture and of our situation, is necessary, and this must be done without panic. The gravity of the situation we are in is great and it is easy to feel too small to do anything. This is why we must break the taboo on inner guidance and should engage in a conversation where we share our deep intuitions publicly. We may consider that we can't wait for science to understand this manner of thinking before using it. It is not perfect, but it is often the best tool that we have. We also must hold awareness as a group and reflect as a group using our best resources. To understand how difficult it is to change without a collective effort, we need to get in touch with our attachment to believing we are individuals.

Individualism

Individualism, which I will discuss along with the closely related idea of independence, is the most openly criticised of the major attachments that I have mentioned. I cannot say individualism is more important than our attachment to rationality because it is so intimately intertwined with rationality.

The idea of the free individual came to prominence during the Enlightenment, and has become a cornerstone of our system of law and morality.[58] It is based on obvious facts: we are clearly separate from each other in some sense; we cannot read each other's mind, or make each other's hands and feet move by an act of will. Starting from this foundation, we have moved a long way towards conceiving of ourselves and our societies as made up of truly independent and equal individuals, freely pursuing our happiness. Though this way of seeing things has produced many amazing and desirable things, it has been a simplifying abstraction, an idealisation or theory. Like all good theories, it is a useful model and guide. However, it is essential not to confuse the model with 'actuality'. Unfortunately, we have done this, with problematic consequences.

The idea of a truly independent individual is an idea that only makes sense to a mind that is determined to be analytical, splitting the world into parts. Humans are clearly made to intertwine with each other.

We live in huge groups and interact with a large number of our fellow species compared to other animals, and it is a good bet that our large brains are made to deal with social reality. As Robin Dunbar has noted, the percentage of an animal's body that is devoted to its brain is very closely related to the size of its social group. The more social a creature, the bigger brain it tends to have.

We get our feelings and ideas largely from each other – people who live near one another have a tendency to think very similar things, which is curious, if we think for ourselves. We automatically (though imperfectly) tend to empathically share subjective experiences with others, which allows us to share feelings, and to take guesses at others' inner lives, and these co-arise with widespread mirroring activity in our brains. If we are not part of a community, we get lonely, deteriorate mentally and die younger.

We also are physically unimpressive as single creatures, and yet, if you go into the wild, you'll find that big carnivores, including lions, have little interest in you. It is not because their ancestral experience tells them a lone man with a spear is a great threat, and it isn't because we don't taste good. It is because humans work together, and if you pick a fight with one human, you pick a fight with their tribe. Lions' instincts tell them to do something else. Our economies and consumption are built on trade with each other, which in turn depends on rules that we collectively enforce through our governments.

The sanctity of the individual and pursuit of desire

Given all this, it is interesting to ask how Westerners convinced themselves of their status as free and independent individuals. The answer seems to lie in the human tendency to turn mere ideas into reality, and the power that the idea of individuality affords to a wide group of people to do what we want without feeling too obligated to either rulers or peers.

The alternative to a free individual, from the perspective of the law, is legal authority of one person over another, as was the case historically in most societies. Kings and patriarchs have in many places and times virtually owned the souls of those of lower status and often could do what they willed with them. Marriages were often arranged, and indentured servitude and slavery were common institutions. The idea that all humans are individuals with equal rights before the law was a concept that grew from the idea of moral equality of people inherent in Christianity (consistent with many mystical traditions) which is explored in the next chapter.[59] This conception of equality is helpful when arguing that humans' earthly interests and ability to make individual choices should be treated as equally important. Such ideas slowly arose during the Middle Ages, and amplified to revolutionary proportions during the Enlightenment era. In order for us to be able to have little obligation to each other, it helps to see our interests as separate, so that is how we see them.

The movement towards individual self-determination based on equal rights created freer societies where people could choose their life path and partners, and more freely invent, innovate and take risks: a society built on free choice, free speech and free trade. It enables pioneers to leave their families and pursue their fortunes, careers and so on.

Strangely, for individualists, we seek to win the admiration of our peers via our accomplishments (see next section).

Experimental evidence shows individualist distortions

Some readers may think that I am overblowing the importance or uniqueness of individualist ideology, so it is useful to review some findings from experimental psychology.

Western psychology found, back in the 1960s, that humans tend to attribute behaviour to the character or talents of individuals, rather than to the situations in which individuals find themselves. This was called the *fundamental attribution error*. An example of this is explaining joblessness in terms of laziness rather than the lack of good jobs, or explaining criminal behaviour in terms of poor moral fibre, rather than situational factors, like family history and the presence of gangs in a neighbourhood.

Around the same time, science had produced very convincing demonstrations that this is not really the case, for example Stanley Milgram's famous conformity experiments. These experiments involved subjects going to a laboratory to participate in what they were told was an experiment in learning. Their job was to read lists to another person, called 'the learner' during the experiment, who would repeat the list back to them. The catch was that subjects were to deliver an electric shock to the learner when an error in learning the list was made. The level of shock would increase after every error. The experiments showed that when instructed by a person of sufficient authority, the vast majority of participants would deliver increasing levels of shock to a person they did not know or see (but heard over an intercom) each time this person was unable to learn lists of symbols appropriately. The 'shocked' people were actually tape recorded but participants did not know this, and the 'shocked' persons begged participants to stop. Most subjects delivered the shock to a point of rendering the person unconscious (maybe dead). In other experimental conditions reported by Milgram, where the experimental subjects could see the person they were supposed to be shocking (played by an actor), few people shocked the subject to unconsciousness. The situation seemed to matter as much as, or more than, the free choices of independent individuals.[60]

But, as mentioned, it seemed to early Western psychologists that 'people' did not recognise the importance of situations. As a teacher of psychology, I can vouch that this is evident in the classroom. Even after watching tape recordings of parts of Milgram's experiment, and reviewing the results in detail, many Western students express astonishment at what monsters the subjects were. A majority of the class raise their hand when asked if they would be one of the few defiant experimental subjects who refused to shock the experimenter (recent replications of Milgram's study show the results are quite similar on contemporary subjects[61]).

The tendency to ignore the situation began to change when psychologists studied other cultures. Conformity has been shown in a number of cultures, but when asked to *explain* the behaviour of conformists, such as Milgram's subjects, East Asian cultures much more often correctly attributed behaviours to aspects of the situation. It turns out that the 'fundamental attribution error' is primarily a Western phenomenon.[62]

Westerners show a number of other differences in experiments that betray a unique sense of the individual and his autonomy. For example, when asked to describe themselves, Westerners, and particularly those who are educated and well-off, are likely to talk about the traits that distinguish themselves from others, such as 'organised', 'hard-working' and 'tough'. In contrast, most other cultures tend to explain themselves in terms of their relationships with others, such as 'daughter', 'teacher' or 'good friend'.[63] Westerners also show a preference for distinguishing themselves. To take just one of many examples, when asked to pick a pen out of a box with many of one colour and one of a second colour, rich Westerners tend to pick the unusual colour, while members of most cultures pick the same.[64]

Thinking for yourself

We often hear it said that people come to their conclusions independently. John Maynard Keynes skewered this idea well:

> Practical men who believe themselves to be quite exempt from any intellectual influence, are usually the slaves of some defunct economist. Madmen in authority, who hear voices in the air, are distilling their frenzy from some academic scribbler of a few years back.[65]

The psychological results above underline Keynes' point. Did our society, and especially its elites, all just happen to independently reach the same conclusions, which have not been reached by other cultures? Anything is possible, but it seems much more likely that we, like all humans, imitate each other relentlessly, getting not only our mannerisms, postures, accents and gaits from each other, but also our feelings about jokes and ideas.

We get particularly good insight into the way that we acquire our feelings about ideas during a common but still strange moment: somebody tells us a joke and we find ourselves laughing, but then realise that we didn't hear the punchline. We must accept, in this case, that we are laughing because other people are laughing. And this suggests that all of the other times when we laughed and *did* hear the punchline, we were *also* affected by others' response. But we have an individualist story with which to make sense of the experience: we heard the joke and independently felt that it was funny.

But does the influence of others on our emotions stop with jokes? Obviously not: in general, we become woven together into a group consciousness, all becoming receptive to one another's emotional reactions to what is said, whether that reaction is laughter, anger or sadness. This happens in groups, and we are not conscious of it (see Kavanagh and Winkielman 2016 for a review[66]). We feel convinced together as surely as we laugh together.

This process has led us to have strong feelings about ideas that, often, we've never really thought about. Our worldview is inherited, but without either knowing a little history or interacting with others who see things differently, this is hard to realise. It is easy to suppose that our view is just the way things are. Our discourse and legal system simply assume individualism, leaving it as little considered as a choice in accent or posture.

It is important to remember, here, the distinction between true insight and merely intellectual knowledge that I mentioned earlier. I notice that the type of reader who is interested in 'take-away messages' doesn't seem much affected by the above – after all, some have said, we all know that culture is received. But we often *say* we know this, and then go right back to talking about how free thinking we are. It is important to watch our minds carefully so that we can deeply convince ourselves that we think together and believe together: we 'inter-feel', 'inter-react', 'inter-believe' and have 'inter-convictions'.

It is only if we really accept this that we will do the work necessary to imagine an alternative society. If we are surrounded by others who think in a different way than we do, then every contact with them can create a feeling of conflict, as if our innate tendency to empathically recreate each other's experience becomes dissonant with the dream we are holding on to. To entertain a dream of a different world is to take on the possibility of suffering when we talk to others who do not share it, and making them suffer from contact with our dreams.

One answer has been to live a lonely life of a dreamer isolated or insulated from the world and most people by a cocoon of inward looking. If dreamers get attached to dreams that require others, and then compare the dream in their mind's eye with the imperfect world in front of them, it is easy to get angry – to get angry with the others who must change, to get upset or to get depressed. The amount of upset becomes greater with the levels of attachment and radicality of the dream, and the more we dare to dream of a world that is different, the more we are open to suffering. When we share a dream with others, we are offering both hope and suffering as well.

One response to our current situation is surely to accept that we cannot dream, hold awareness, or envision and act with full effectiveness *alone*. We can start to remedy loneliness by holding *both* the knowledge of the ways things are; *and* the knowledge that others do not want the pain that comes with believing in a radically different world. That is the best place from which to convince others to dream.

Loneliness is a shadow of individualism

Old people watching their children disappear over the horizon, going away on a great adventure to become greater, is a frequent scene in movies that explore our shared fantasy of striking out and making it. Movies don't typically linger long on the parents who remain behind, just as we don't look often at retirement homes.

Popular songs also pay homage to the individualist spirit. Frank Sinatra's 'My Way', Bobby Brown's 'My Prerogative', and Rascal Flatts 'Life is a Highway' all conjure up and glorify the image of a self-determined life, and the pop star is an archetype of the free-spirited individualist, flamboyant and unique. Musicians focus on distinguishing themselves from their peers and ancestors, rather than bowing to community and tradition.

The rise of individuality has been helped along by its consonance with consumerism and careerism. If joy stems from accomplishments and things, rather than people, then it is easier for us to be a world of people doing exactly what we want, independent of each other's actions. Then, of course we'd be in control, free to make plans and choices and life would be easier to figure out – and other people, complex and unpredictable, just get in the way.

On the other hand, if we need each other, true independence is a strange idea. John Lennon famously said that 'life is what happens when you're making other plans'. He was reflecting on relationships with other humans who have their own desires. Broken hearts, loneliness, the healing effects of community, the need to take care of others, people feeling depressed because nobody is coming to their party, and so on are familiar phenomena that give the lie to 'independence' and make planning hard.

This contradiction between ideals and nature explains why there are so many songs written by rebels loudly proclaiming to the world how little they care. Ironically, it often feels important to them to convince the people whose opinions they don't care about.

This tension between romantic notions of individuality plays out with disturbing regularity in daily lives – famously in romance. We need to acknowledge bonds with one another for romance and sex – and to have children. And so then, when a union is formed and children are had, independence, we often hear it said, is surrendered. In theory, two people become one person, and the united couple make their independent life choices, moving far away for better jobs and better weather, and so on. Many people still spend their time complaining bitterly about their loss of freedom in marriage. Much has been made of the great divorce rates in the contemporary West and the unwillingness to take the needs of a partner into consideration and compromise – acting like an individual is high on the list. Another frequently remarked on problem is the pressure that is placed on marriage because couples find themselves alone without a wider network of family and friends.

Individualism in the politics of climate change

Rhetoric of individual consumer choices

The first way in which individualism manifests in terms of the climate crisis is the credulity with which we often hear individual consumption choices discussed as a realistic route to halting climate change. On the climate activist side, the rhetoric of individual choice is not absolute, but it is overblown, and some climate activists genuinely seem to believe their goals can be accomplished through consumer choices. More importantly, climate sceptics somehow manage to claim, in argument after argument, that total freedom from individual 'carbon sin' is a standard by which they can judge the sincerity of activists' climate concerns. They cast their opponents as hypocrites if they so much as own a television, and somehow few of us laugh at the absurdity of this view.[67]

Let's remind ourselves of the inherent collectivity of the climate crisis – each individual, acting alone, can do little to affect their own environment. I could on the one hand take a plane and fly around the Earth in circles, fuelling in mid-air for the rest of my life; or on the other hand, I could stay on a small patch of land working it with a hand hoe, and my choice will make no difference at all to my personal experience of climate change.

So, if people are a little bit selfish, each will tend to indulge himself, and do damage to the Earth that we all must share. And so we will all share a very damaged Earth. It would be admirable for us to cultivate such love of others that we'd act with no distinction between our welfare and that of all of nature, including humanity. It is foolish to bet our survival on this, and that is precisely what we do when we wait for individual choices to drive down emissions. This kind of situation is exactly why laws and rules are created, and can be beneficial, even in the most traditional societies. Sharing of common resources (such as shared food in a family) without formal arrangements works within the context of a community with strong ties and strong values around protecting these common resources, but these ties don't exist across the whole world.[68]

I am not saying that cutting down on one's personal carbon footprint as a matter of conscience is a bad or foolish thing; it sets a good example by showing others that a low carbon life can be enjoyable. It also makes one a more credible communicator in a culture of individualism that will cling on to any reason to dismiss those who urge carbon neutrality. But it is not a workable solution to sharing our Earth.

What, therefore, is a more clear-eyed way of viewing our individual responsibility to a world that does not have the collective agreements it needs to control emissions? If our culture were made up of people who saw themselves as inter-being, as part of a vast collective, we would think in terms of what we could do to bring down emissions as a whole society. The problem comes once we start seeing ourselves as one small part of a large chain of causation. In practice, activists are forced to think this way, to travel long distances to engage with other activists, to plan strategy, lobby politically and so on. The process of political change within an effective timescale requires actions that require carbon. Why should climate be different?

Yes, like everybody, climate activists will lie to themselves. They will justify emissions that a perfect person would not make. The lack of perfect people is exactly why we need laws in large societies. This shows the exasperating vapidness of our discourse. We somehow manage to make it commonplace to discredit people, activists, who are saying that we all need help to nudge our behaviour into a more healthy direction, for demonstrating that they, too, need that help. On some level, it makes about as much sense as discrediting an advocate for forming an Alcoholics Anonymous group by saying that he shouldn't be talking about others drinking because he drinks himself. The notion of change may be correct, but conversation always transforms into a matter of who is better than the other, rather than about achieving action.

So we can't proudly say that we act while thinking on a collective level because in our societies we are judged as individuals, and we are judged by actions whose effects are 'objective', rather than subjective. So, for example, the positive effects of attending a meeting are 'subjective', while the emissions from travel are not, and so an objective, individualist perspective is more strongly rooted than a subjective, social perspective. The individualist consideration simply feels more real because of ideology. The climate problem requires a social-level approach. We as a society will make choices that will determine the future, even if those choices are to make no new laws and suffer the consequences.

Libertarian streaks

Libertarianism is an extreme version of individualist sentiment, which claims to advance freedom by forbidding us to write laws that tell individuals what to do. Libertarians believe that society and markets will organise themselves as a matter of individual choices. We will be able to share the space well while all doing what we want. This ideology is present in a less strong form in various statements of business interest.

The reality is that our choices interfere with others' choices and we avoid awareness of this only by dogma. As George Bernard Shaw noted, a smoker and a non-smoker cannot have the same rights on a train car, and so laws like banning smoking emissions make sense. The climate crisis is quite like a global train car, except that the greatest polluters feel the effects the least – scientific projections are that it is mostly homes near the equator that will become uninhabitable within decades.

By stopping the US from taking part in solutions, political parties who are most rigidly built around the sanctity of individual freedoms have ensured global inaction on climate. All along, they've spoken the language of the collective 'interfering' with the individual's freedom: an idea which only really makes sense if we assume individuals have a natural state of existence that is independent of laws. If there is such a state, it is something like one hunter-gatherers live in. Societies with the complex systems of industry and range of choices that we have are all based on laws.

It is worth noting that the US is the most famously and fiercely individualistic nation on earth, and it is the only place where libertarianism has a broad following – though other countries have streaks of this ideology. This is not a coincidence. Libertarianism is the belief that essentially we don't need a government because individuals acting on their own will solve problems. Libertarianism is famously influential in Silicon Valley,[69] because in the absence of collective action we tend to see technology (e.g. Bitcoin, Tesla) as the solution to our problems. If individual inventors acting alone can solve our problems, then no government is necessary. If an inventor can, through brilliance, make clean energy cheaper than high-carbon energy, then no government is necessary. And so libertarian individualists are drawn to technological solutions to collective problems, and technologists find the libertarian worldview agreeable.

Questioning equality?

> Equality is not a source of suffering, but the equality complex is
>
> *Thich Nhat Hanh*[70]

Of all the Enlightenment ideas to which the West is attached, equality most resembles the teaching of a slowly fraying, organised religion, with all its buried wisdom and strained rhetoric. Like many religions, our gospel of equality had its start in a precious insight – into the unity of human lives – but we say things in the name of equality that are rather strange, and questioning these statements might get you excommunicated (or cancelled). What is greatest about our sense of equality is beyond words, but often efforts to speak about it clearly end up sowing confusion.

I'll recount a few examples of dogmas. When I was a schoolchild, my classmates and I were told that 'you can do anything you want, if you set your mind to it!' It seemed strange when I looked at the giants who played American football and basketball. When I went to college, I remember running into a few people who felt that being a feminist meant denying differences in size and strength between males and females. And more and more I've heard it objected that 'you can't generalise!' when seemingly any statement is made about differences between groups. At the same time, I have heard that all lives are of equal value while being disturbed by how little news of the deaths of Iraqis and Afghans affected Americans during wars waged in those countries compared to news of our own troops' deaths. All of these are examples of how our ideas about equality affect our day-to-day life while being out of line with the way things are.

There are good reasons why we've held on to this ideal, while Piss Christs and shock entertainment have almost exhausted their ability to offend us.[71] Equality is at the absolute centre of our moral life, and has been central to social movements that have improved the lives of almost all demographics. Most of our ancestors were serfs or were enslaved at the time of the Enlightenment, and did not become equal enough to vote until the 19th or 20th centuries. Equality was at the core of their appeal as they advanced their position.

The point of this chapter is to question our notions of equality seriously, but not to argue that 'equality is a bad idea'. Rather, our conversations about equality are too badly confused to be called right or wrong. Our notions of equality have one of their roots in a timeless insight into the unity of humanity, which is seldom seen clearly and never captured with words. Around this has grown a maze of ideas, some noble and some misguided, that are supposed to guide humans to act consistently with deep truth. Like similar attempts in religion, where this has involved creating simplistic dogmas and taboos, it has gone sour.

The ideal of the equality of humans has also gained its authority *by having a great deal of truth*; 99.9 per cent of humans' genes are the same as one another, so we all have eight billion virtual copies of ourselves scattered around the planet. Our sense of this similarity expresses itself most powerfully in spirituality and art, and it is called for in these uncertain times.

But, unfortunately, one of our many common features is fixation on the few differences that separate us. Paradoxically, the most confused dogmas around equality have spread because it has been hoped that by denying differences, society could be stopped from organising around them. These dogmas seem to be imagined as stones set in place to seal a vault containing the dark forces of difference: tribalism, nationalism, sexism and othering of all kinds.

For as long as I can remember, I have felt that this was a wrong way of looking at things, that the impulses beneath othering cannot be denied (as literature, science and unspeakable acts by human groups against one another attest to), and it is better to admit and engage with them openly.[72] But it was just too arrogant and uncomfortable to suggest a course of action that amounted to moving the stone. There seemed to be such confidence that these forces were being suffocated by being denied air, and there seemed to be some signs that this was true: civil rights victories, a Black president, more people of colour in more visible and high-status roles, and so on. I feel it is now time to admit that this project has been pursued long enough to conclude that it has deep flaws which are not going away. At the same time, there is surely enough truth behind our notion of equality to motivate ourselves to treat each other better than we have done till now.

The two equalities

It is important at the outset, to distinguish between two related but distinct notions of equality: the notion that all lives are equally sacred, which I will call 'deep equality', and the idea that people are or should be equal in valued opportunities, outcomes and traits, which I will call 'surface equalities'. These distinctions between these senses of equality, I think, are far more important and far more confused than is commonly supposed. The tension between them maps onto our ego's tendency to see others in terms of the characteristics that set them apart from us while our mystic sense is attuned to our unity. The confusion between these two senses of the word are key to understanding why we've developed such tension around equality.

Deep equality

The equal sacredness of human lives is often expressed by the statement 'we are all equal in the eyes of God' – a Christian idea that made its way into Enlightenment philosophy. The heritage of this idea was eloquently articulated by Martin Luther King in his sermon on 'The American Dream':

> This morning I would like to deal with some of the
> challenges that we face today in our nation as a result of
> the American dream. First, I want to reiterate the fact that
> we are challenged more than ever before to respect the
> dignity and the worth of all human personality. We are
> challenged to really believe that all men are created equal.
> And don't misunderstand that. It does not mean that all
> men are created equal in terms of native endowment,
> in terms of intellectual capacity – it doesn't mean that.
> There are certain bright stars in the human firmament in
> every field ... What it does mean is that all men are equal
> in intrinsic worth.
>
> You see, the founding fathers were really influenced
> by the Bible. The whole concept of the imago dei, as
> it is expressed in Latin, the 'image of God', is the idea

that all men have something within them that God injected. Not that they have substantial unity with God, but that every man has a capacity to have fellowship with God. And this gives him a uniqueness, it gives him worth, it gives him dignity. And we must never forget this as a nation: there are no gradations in the image of God. Every man from a treble white to a bass black is significant on God's keyboard.[73]

The first paragraph is very natural to read within a secular mindset, but in the second, King turns to theology. This is not only because King was a religious man, but because the feeling behind this paragraph is impossible to ground in a way that does not strain past the limits of rationality.

The Christian contemplative Thomas Merton describes the same insight in slightly less religious language:

In Louisville, at the corner of Fourth and Walnut, in the center of the shopping district, I was suddenly overwhelmed with the realisation that I loved all those people, that they were mine and I theirs, that we could not be alien to one another even though we were total strangers. It was like waking from a dream of separateness, of spurious self-isolation in a special world, the (monastic) world of renunciation and supposed holiness .... This sense of liberation from an illusory difference was such a relief and such a joy to me that I almost laughed out loud .... I have the immense joy of being man, a member of a race in which God Himself became incarnate. As if the sorrows and stupidities of the human condition could overwhelm me, now I realize what we all are. And if only everybody could realize this! But it cannot be explained. There is no way of telling people that they are all walking around shining like the sun.[74]

It is easy for me to agree with Merton that he is describing something that most of us merely only glance in flickers of intense camaraderie, before being drawn back to our own form of self-isolation. As a person who does not believe in the Christian God, I find that I can see the notion of equality in the eyes of God as a metaphor, in which I see all humans as children of some creator, whether that is God or the universe. It is a metaphor that invites me to inhabit a 'God's eye view' from which I see others and myself like a loving parent would see their many children: all unique, and all equally loved.

But as Merton says, much like other states that tend to be discussed as spiritual or sacred, no words can quite capture this deep sense of equality unless we have already intensely noticed it in our direct experience. What Merton's words arouse in me, at least, is a yearning to see this thing, which I've sometimes glimpsed, more fully and more often myself, rather than a greater understanding of what it is like to see others this way. I don't think it is very different from what Buddhists mean by insight into 'no self' and so I am inspired to contemplation rather than to further descriptions.

So it is sometimes better to simply talk about this inherent dignity as 'self-evident', as did the framers of the US Declaration of Independence. It is clearly not *that* self-evident or else we would not need governments and rights to make us act as though we saw it clearly. We can, at best, call it 'potentially self-evident' to everybody, and perhaps truly self-evident only to those who manage to see what Merton saw, often after years of practice. But still today the universal Declaration of Human Rights states this equality as though it were obvious: 'recognition of the *inherent* dignity and of the equal and inalienable rights of all members of the human family' (Ishay 1997: 407, italics mine). Few people will dare to openly disagree. This not only has much to do with shared but imperfect insight into what Merton said, but also with ego-driven politics, which I will be in a better position to explain after addressing the second sense of equality below.

Surface equalities

The second sense of equality is more seemingly straightforward. It might be talked about more clearly as equality in terms of 'surface characteristics', such as income, education, work rights and even talents. I've chosen the name surface equality more because these dimensions are more easily visible than because they are less important than deep equality. Surface equalities might seem quite distinct from deep equality, but these ideas get mixed together for a number of reasons, discussed below.

Rules about surface equality are meant to address ethical and moral questions in ways that are consistent with deep equality, and that are clear, codifiable and 'actionable'. For example, how should political influence be spread? Equally, one person equals one vote. What should every person's chances of being drafted to war be? Equal. What opportunity should people have to go to college? Equal. Some societies influenced by enlightenment traditions have gone further, declaring that income and ownership of capital should also be equal. Debates over whether this clear answer was actually right have consumed a lot of time and resulted in bloodbaths.

Equality of opportunity and equality of outcome

It is a relatively straight line, logically, from the notion that all lives are equally sacred to the idea that a society should conduct itself so that the happiness and suffering of all people is equally weighted in its decisions. But straight lines from this principle to specific behaviour are seldom easy to draw. Two notable attempts at generally applicable principles that might guide us are known as *equality of outcomes* and *equality of opportunity*.

Equality of outcomes is intuitively attractive: if humans really loved each other like dear friends, they would share possessions like one big happy family, there would be little in the way of abject poverty, and so on. Things should be divided so that all are equally satisfied. Some need more than others, of course, but this is hard to determine, so we often go with the rough-and-ready heuristic of equality.

We can see this idea in action when a close group of friends divides up a set amount of a thing that everybody wants. When the proverbial pizza is divided consciously and deliberately in front of a watchful group of friends, it tends to be done equally. We often pay equally or try to divide the work of making pizza equally. But as soon as the relationships of people are less close, pizza is scarce, there are too many pizzas and people to keep track of, or some people get there earlier than others, then idealism is challenged. Either unfair pizza division happens or we must count out slices equally with all people present to watch. Most importantly, if the cooking or buying of these pizzas is consistently left to a few people, the pizza tends to stop being made. It is generally acknowledged that everybody being equally well fed is the best outcome, but getting there is a challenge in a society of imperfect people.

Equality of opportunity is often the more morally pragmatic approach to embrace when we notice that getting people to make things in the first place is the hard part of creating a world with adequate pizza. We don't have to divide the total amount made equally, but we can give people a (truly) equal chance to get enough pizza.

In order for the pizza analogy to fit the circumstances of our society, we can imagine a huge group of people (hundreds?) at a group outing where there are enough raw ingredients and ovens to make enough pizza for everybody – but the task of making and dividing pizza is too large to be coordinated as one group. We'd organise into small groups (like society's families), each of which would make their own pizza and divide it fairly equally among themselves. The people who did more work might feel entitled to take more, and those who were better prepared to make pizza will feel pulled to share their work and to teach others. Very likely, a lot more pizza would get made in this situation, than if hundreds of people, unknown to each other, felt equally entitled to whichever pizza came out of the oven. And if somebody was left out as the ovens and ingredients were occupied by others, those others might feel drawn to give the left-out person some pizza to make up for their lack of opportunity. Or perhaps those who had got there first would decide that whoever had been left out had simply not made the most of their opportunity. Either way, their thoughts will include the ideal of equality of opportunity.

These two conceptions of surface equality influence policy and distribution of goods in complex ways. Communist and socialist societies, for example, could be described as having greater commitment to equality of outcome, while pure capitalist societies emphasise equality of opportunity. Western countries typically show aspects of both of these views, which is sensible because they are simply theories about desirable outcomes, imperfect like all theories. Both are just ways of creating simple heuristics that we can follow (and make each other follow), thereby approximating outcomes at which a society of complete kindness would naturally arrive.

The concepts underlying surface equality discussions

In addition to *outcome* and *opportunities*, conversations about equality rely on several ideas: the *merits* people have, which include their *talents* and (moral) *character*.[75] These ideas together form the guts of our meritocratic ideology, and we cannot make sense of our conversations about equality without understanding them.

The standard definitions of these terms are something like this: opportunities are the chances we have in life to achieve something; outcomes (or achievements) are what we actually manage to obtain, and merits are our abilities to achieve, shown by how much we turn opportunity into outcomes. Merit can be broken down into two parts, though this becomes controversial: talents are the abilities given to us by nature or God; our character is shown by the extent to which we apply our talents to the opportunities presented, to do the best we can. Whether character or talent is more important for determining merits is a great (unwinnable) debate, but talent and character together are seen as determining how we turn opportunities into outcomes.

I do not claim that these ideas are 'right'. However, together with equality of opportunity, these ideas form an intellectual system that our society uses to help groups, from simple families to whole societies, decide who is best at taking actions and who has earned praise, attention and rewards. They are also intellectual inventions that excite our egos, which want all of the rewards that come when our merits are acknowledged by others and by ourselves. Just like the notion of the self, these ways of thinking are practical, but they may not be as deeply true as our habitual use of them tends to make us believe.

Judgements about what levels various people have of these characteristics are highly subjective, and it is often asked what these categories mean. For example, is piano-playing ability a talent or an outcome of hard work? Or, can character 'make its own opportunities'? I will leave these questions for others to answer. My point is simply that surface equalities related to the above dimensions are central to the way we justify our society and are shaped by arguments as much as by 'the facts'.

Dimensions of surface equality are relative

It is worth underlining the relative nature of these dimensions. We mainly discuss a person's talents, characteristics, opportunities and outcomes that 'stand out' relative to other people's. People are not, for example, proud of being smart unless they are especially smart compared to somebody else. People do not become envious of an opportunity or outcome that literally everyone else has, but they can be very envious of one that everybody but them has. We also merit attention, raises and vacations relative to others. For this reason, all discussion related to merits is political and influenced by the drives of various egos for recognition.

The conflation of the two senses of equality

Surface equalities might seem quite distant from deep equality, but these ideas get mixed together for a number of reasons.

The first of these is easy to understand. We often tend to get ideas with the same name mixed up ('being right' versus 'being within your rights'), and such confusion is helped along when two senses of the world are deeply related even though they are quite distinct (see below).

Second, equality in outcomes and opportunities tends to increase with appreciation of deep equality. In a world where we all felt deep equality as clearly as King and Merton, there would be far greater surface equality. Nobody who wanted a house, a meal or a community would be without one. We would instinctively send our efforts and resources down the avenues that would lead to the greatest human flourishing. We would see greater equality in outcomes because an extra slice of bread or a blanket is a generally greater source of joy to the person who has little, and the person who has more will tend to miss these less.

Third, in many cases, the 'objective' measure of a 'subjective' thing becomes spoken about more than the thing it measures because it is easier to grasp. Money is easily equated with 'living standards' because money can be grasped easily and it is correlated with better living standards.[76] Likewise, the ability to stretch further is seen as a measure of a yoga practitioner's ability because stretching is more visible than the inner discipline that produces it. This stretching tends to become identified with yogic ability.

Fourth, the objectivity of surface equality also makes it easier to fake. We can more convincingly pretend to love someone as we do ourselves than we can pretend to pay them an equal amount of money as we pay ourselves. This means that discussion of surface equality can feel more real.

Fifth, when we fail to appreciate deep equality, we distort our views of each other's talents, opportunities and outcomes to make an image of the world that gives a place of privilege to our own merits. We tend to construct and promote stories about our life that minimise the role of opportunities and maximise the role of talent and character in the results we obtain. This means exaggerating the opportunities of others relative to our own as much as we can without our story being cut down by facts.

Sixth, emphasis on deep equality, the lucid appreciation of all that we have in common, falls within territory that is traditionally called spiritual, or religious, and it has become taboo to discuss politics while standing in religious territory. Thus, public debate tends to focus on surface equality, rather than dwelling on the appreciation of deep equality that can drive it.

Equality as dogma

Allow me to experientially demonstrate how much of a taboo has developed around questioning equality. Please consider statements of the form: 'X is not a source of suffering, but an obsession with X is.' For example:

Money is not a source of suffering, but an obsession with money is.

Achievement is not a source of suffering, but an obsession with achievement is.

Being good-looking is not a source of suffering, but an obsession with being good-looking is.

There are many things that do not cause suffering, but an obsession with anything is a source of suffering.

My experience is that most people would agree with these. However, many get uncomfortable if I say:

Equality is not a source of suffering, but an obsession with equality is.

Which is just a slightly paraphrased version of a statement by the Zen Master, Thich Nhat Hanh that I started this chapter with:

Equality is not a source of suffering, but the equality complex is.

It is the only statement of his that I have often seen raise people's defences. I should clarify that he is talking here about obsession with surface equality (income, chances to speak, etc.). He is not trying to say we shouldn't notice inequalities or respond to them; it only means that if we are attached to seeing equality, then suffering will surely follow. It is worth noting that people don't have nearly the same reaction to inserting 'rational explanation' or 'individual freedom' into the blanks above. People seldom object to inserting any other good thing in the blank. But we are more unapologetically obsessed with equality than with other foundations of the Western mindset.

How equality obsession makes us suffer

All obsessions make us suffer, but in different ways: the most unique suffering that comes from an obsession with equal levels of opportunity or outcomes is a disruption of our ability to experience ourselves as part of a 'we' – a sense which actually lies at the base of deep equality.

Of course, when division of resources, respect, attention and rights moves towards equality, suffering often lessens. As the quote says, 'Equality is not a source of suffering…'. Questioning the health of an equality obsession does not mean forgetting about surface equalities, but rather indicates finding a healthy relationship with our awareness of them. We can pay attention to surface equality and appreciate deep equality at the same time, but not if we become totally fixated on differences in outcomes and opportunities and the reasons for them. A quest to eliminate differences (create equality) often leads us to live in a world of differences.[77] To put it in more familiar terms, comparing our level of social status with others tends to put us 'in our head', separate from others, and yet the ability for 'heart-to-heart' connection is most important for actually taking many of the most difficult moral actions. This is especially true when such actions require sacrifice, which will most easily be undertaken when we see deeply that all lives are worthy of concern and respect. Dealing with an obsession with our ideals of equality is hard because, like those obsessed with cleaning or food, just forgetting about the object of our obsession is not an option.

How did we get to be so obsessed with surface equality?

One major reason for our obsession has been discussed already: surface equality and deep equality have become merged into one confused whole. Western society knows, at some level, that its ideas about equality are messy, but it relies on these ideas, and sees no better alternative. The natural reaction to the questioning of any statements that we are not confident in is defensiveness and anger. The amount of defensiveness around discussion of equality stops confusion from being pointed out and so the conversation is stagnant. The confusion allows us to treat demands for greater surface equality as though they had equal moral gravitas as building a world of sisters and brothers. This confidence holds even when equality is spoken for with a disdainful sense of moral superiority, which makes our society more and more a family divided.

An obvious alternative approach is to cultivate appreciation of deep equality directly, which can never be done disdainfully. This route, though, is barred by a distrust in its efficacy based on historical experience. This part of our evolution of equality obsession may need a little more explanation.

I can start this explanation by returning to the objections that I receive when repeating Thich Nhat Hanh's quote. In my experience, when people hear the Zen Master talk about suffering that can come from the equality complex, they become puzzled or intrigued, but when I repeat these words, they often say something like, 'but we can't just accept massive inequality!'

I *could* reply: if a person says, 'I think being obsessed with looking good causes me suffering', we do not assume that she means, 'I'm going to just accept looking terrible.' Analogously, by questioning an obsession with equality, I am not passively accepting extreme inequality.

But, of course, this response would not address the source of many people's suspicions about where I'm headed with my talk of equality complexes. I am a white male Zen non-master, with unearned privileges in Western society, which is privileged relative to the whole world. Many would reasonably suspect me of using Thich Nhat Hanh's quote to build an argument in favour of preserving these privileges. They might suspect that I am trying to open the door to the possibility that others should be satisfied with my continued enjoyment of unearned privileges, rather than trying to address our very real problems from a place of compassion. If even this simple quote arouses such suspicions, then the equality conversation will never go anywhere without addressing these concerns.

Representing white males

At this point, I feel it is appropriate to discuss how my identity impacts my feelings on this point directly. Personally, I feel that as long as I, and other white males, are selfish (have egos), there will always be good reasons for the suspicions that a white man's way of addressing ideological rigidities around equality will be more passive acceptance of unfairness, rather than intelligent, subtle and deep concern. White men will experience a pull towards being defensive and ignorant of how we are advantaged, and why others distrust us. Being ignorant seems like an easy way to feel at peace with the current situation, and the past. But as long as we have eyes and ears and a moral sense, we'll be uneasy around the gap between our lifestyles and that of others.

Speaking collectively, if white men's high ideals of equality were matched by deep conviction, then we, and Westerners, generally, would be making much more serious plans to share our wealth. As it is, Western nations could not accept groups of refugees that made up less than two per cent of their populations, and our efforts to help other countries are far from the centre of national attention.

So how can I question equality when my people, white men, have a record of holding onto power? The truth is, we would have a lot to lose if either outcome or opportunity equality were somehow mandated tomorrow across the world. But the truth also is that I personally can honestly say that conversations about equality don't make me feel attacked as a white male, just humbled. Also, though such conversations build a healthy awareness of privilege, they sometimes seem to present me with a stark choice: remain aligned to freedom of enquiry or remain in allegiance to a loose social movement that claims to be creating surface equality. The right to rule of kings was yesterday's dogma and it was questioned, and fell in favour of ideals of equality. So whatever ideals of surface equality have done for humanity in the past, questioning received truth has done more. I will continue with the questioning later, after discussing the humility that knowing history gives me.

Of course, white men used to be taught that they are history's heroes who have done great things for equality, so the truth of our history can hurt. Just like many groups throughout history, white men have used superior technology to create empires, and impose their wills and desires on others. There were many dedicated abolitionists who organised to stop slavery but descendants of the colonised and enslaved are still faced with police brutality and discrimination in the courts. Like almost all people in any time or place, Westerners have not shown total enough belief in equality to give away enough of their money and become equal in financial privileges to others. It does happen, but it is *very* rare.

But another way of looking at the history of equality is that particular groups have fought mostly for their own equality. Once they had obtained legal equality, many groups (starting with rich white men, then poor white men, then women and people of colour in varying order) seemed happy to remain 'more equal than others' (as Orwell put it). Groups such as gay people, or people outside our borders, were still denied many rights, but objections on behalf of those groups have never been as loud as those groups' own. The group of Black lesbian feminists known as the Combahee River Collective, who coined the term 'identity politics', famously remarked on this tendency, which explained why they absolutely had to advocate for their own dignity.[78] The women's rights, civil rights and gay rights movements made gains, but left members of this collective, at the intersection of these three oppressions, still marginalised. Groups that have wanted recognition as equals have often framed their struggles in terms of 'humanity'. But oppressed groups' interest in humanity has waned when their own problems were reduced, though some truly committed individuals have been motivated by a sense of deep equality.

I don't think it is too harsh to say that *the biggest* difference between privileged Westerners and other dominant groups throughout history is that they popularised the practice of groups fighting for *their own* equality with the ruling class, while relying on the stirring language of deep equality for greatest possible rhetorical effect. When we become conscious of this, powerful reactions can arise. The guilt that so many white people express is just one reaction, which is easy to express openly. Other reactions are to decide that our ideals are a joke, and perhaps to hate ourselves or all of humanity for our hypocrisy, to wrap ourselves in nihilism or to cynically conclude that ideas are only weapons to be used to our benefit. Alternatively, we can acknowledge that people whose ancestors struggled for more equal opportunities (which is almost all of us) often have their hearts warmed when they see others succeed in the same way; they just do not share this joy equally.

Mere ideas cannot drive us to those heights of selflessness, so we must come to terms with the fact that we are expecting too much of our ideals. As mentioned previously, humans don't align their hearts with their beliefs easily. To convince ourselves more deeply of our ideals, to make deep convictions out of them and live more consistently with them, we need to question and reflect on them deeply. We need to make a virtue out of seeing deep equality, and practise it every day, and probably to teach it in schools, and not merely as an intellectual subject but a moral one. And still, deep equality would be hard to see.

However we judge the West's past and present, morally, its technological prowess has put it in a position of power and responsibility. For our own good and for everybody else's, Westerners must respond to the climate crisis that we mostly created, but which is affecting the whole world. This process is making the shallowness of Western convictions around equality abundantly clear, and so we will soon have to examine them. We are not equally concerned for our children as for ourselves, much less for people in other countries, and their children. We may start towards a real political response by accepting that all egoic people, which in practice means all people, have a tendency towards selfishness and group egotism that means we care more about ourselves and our kind than about others. This acceptance means that we can stop hating ourselves, but it doesn't mean keeping things as they are, because it doesn't mean ignoring others.

It is the same kind of acceptance that starts off effective engagement with bad, deep habits, such as drinking too much, lying or shoplifting. It allows us to see their roots and effects clearly, without being caught up in guilt and self-hatred. Since the root of our unseriousness about inequality is ego, and letting go of ego seems impossible, without a spirit of acceptance it is easy for privileged Westerners to avoid the subject or attempt to redeem ourselves through professions of guilt or attacking others who are still worse. None of this does much to change our passion-driven habits; all of it feeds ego.

So as a white male, I'd suggest that everybody just accept a few things. Having an ego means you don't want to be equal, but better. Having power (as we usually define it) means that you don't have to be equal if you don't want to be. So, as long as there is power and selfishness, there will not be equality in outcomes or in opportunities. It is doubtful that our equality obsession will change this. At the same time, we can see that ideals of surface equality are a very useful but limited check on power, and that greater love and compassion are possible, as well as necessary, in order to approach our ideals as closely as possible.

Moving from dogma to compassion, for everybody's sake

A pragmatic concern for all humans can guide us to be less reactive about equality. If the environmental movement, or any group, *hatefully* says, 'you must treat all others with complete equality' and either implicitly (through contemptuous tone) or explicitly claims moral superiority, it undermines its own credibility. Only saints really achieve this. By claiming to live up to our ideals of equality, those of us who feel the West must reckon with its historical legacies of colonialism, racism and violence are easily dismissed as hypocrites. Now is not the time to let that happen. We'd do better by embracing *both* ideals about surface equality *and* the compassion for both ourselves and others that many ancient wisdom traditions advocate and that complement deep equality. This is not the tone of many current public conversations, which are not helping to address an ecological disaster that stands to be tragically unequal in its consequences.

The stakes are high – the climate crisis may be so brutal in the choices that it presents to us, that the privileged and well-armed West may find itself letting go of its norms of equality and universalism as it struggles to justify its responses. If we end up replacing egalitarian ideals that we don't live up to with a return to open prejudice, that will be a great tragedy. It is a real possibility that we are still not seriously considering, mostly because we can't enthusiastically imagine the realities of a climate disrupted world.

Taking a loving and compassionate approach is not easy, but it seems to be the only choice. Just as we can easily *act* humble, but not easily *be* humble, it is not easy to cultivate a loving and compassionate way of being. Activism and politics supported by these ways of being often do, however, drive social change better than relying on heavy moralistic appeals to ideals, as shown by the work of great peacemakers of the 20th century such as Gandhi and King.

Love and morality

'Love' and 'morality' are words that can sit awkwardly together. *Morality* is often associated with 'you should', and *love* more associated with 'I accept'. It is commonly thought that accepting others (loving) means letting them behave how they want without intervention, which is inconsistent with taking actions in favour of fairness. Except for children, it is a common sentiment that we should allow people their individual free choice, or else we are 'moralising'.

The kind of *acceptance* that goes along with love is not the same as *approving* of every action a person takes; it does not even imply that we won't try to change their behaviour. Love involves willingness to see into another person, seeing their past, their mindset, their pains, sorrows and joys deeply, and acting with these in mind. We often turn a blind eye to the behaviour of some people that we are affectionate

87

towards, such as a family and friends who cheat on their partner. If we really love them, though, we are more likely to find the courage to say something when they are making a mess of their life.

If one enquires into this relationship between love and clear-sightedness, it is easy to see why love is so hard. Love is intimately tied to awareness. We must accept people and situations to *really* see them. It is easy to love somebody when we like what we become aware of, but when we look at a person and see something that is out of line with our wants or ideals, or is threatening, this is challenging. Our attention flies away from what it senses that it cannot accept, and so we remain ignorant, with our consciousness out of line with things as they are. But we have to see each other more clearly to find our way to the best world that we can.

Meritocracy and equality: a fundamental contradiction

The egoic drive that interferes with compassion and love is timeless, but amplified in our time by meritocratic ideology, which revolves around citizens expressing their potential and distinguishing themselves from one another through 'high performance'. *Though Westerners say we want to be equal, we don't want to be average, and we don't respect average results.* Western societies have often seen themselves as *above* all other societies in history, for allowing their citizens and even 'outsiders' more equal opportunities to achieve to the limit of their abilities. However, the psychological dynamics of meritocracy are fundamentally in tension with our appreciation of deep equality.

Though it is taboo to actually say so, in practice we openly value the talented and hard-working more than others. Culturally, we favour people who we more enjoy looking at, who have nice houses and can give us jobs, who can come up with clever ideas and acts, who easily draw the interest of, and who can manage, others. We pay greater attention to them, including their pain and suffering.[79] Those lower on the status hierarchy, such as the homeless or the mentally ill, do not command our sympathies as much. When a high-profile athlete dies young, it is a national tragedy, but if his lesser-known teammate dies, it will barely be mentioned.

The idea of merit in itself might *seem* out of line with deep equality, but this is exactly what King warned us about. The identification of 'bright stars in the human firmament' can simply be a means for deciding how society should spread its resources so that those who have the greatest potential to contribute to society are nurtured. Think of the choices made by families throughout the world who do not have the resources to provide all of their children with as much schooling as they might like. Such families often pick one person, based on their merits, to invest more in, with the understanding that the person who gets this privilege must then provide for other people. The 'gifted' sibling understands that their schooling was provided in the spirit of community. Great privileges are supposed to come with great responsibilities. But egos grasp at the possibilities that accompany such merit, and that come from being friends with those who are marked as having high merit. So merit simply becomes a new form of status. And conversations about merit become arguments over status.

The myth and decay of meritocracy

If those who receive privileges follow their egoic impulses, they quickly lose their sense of obligation and gratitude to others. So our imperfect meritocracies are often run by privileged men who want to think of themselves as self-made (but who do not wish to pay higher taxes). Neither equality of opportunity nor equality of outcomes is in the narrow interests of powerful people. But it is in the interests of the powerful to insist that meritocracy is functioning well.[80] This means insisting that their positions are deserved, as are the positions of the poor. Meritocracy encourages our ego to strive to bathe in the warm glow of pride that comes with the story that we did it ourselves. No conspiracy of the powerful is even necessary to create a false myth of meritocracy; the powerful will do it by virtue of their amplified influence and by having the same kind of vanity that everybody else has.

Still, the whole dynamic of our meritocracy depends on people being able to confidently devote themselves to achieving and dreaming, which depends on a genuine pursuit of surface equalities by society. The contradictions between meritocratic ideals and realities mean that there is plenty of room for people to save meritocratic progress by advocating for greater equality of opportunity and outcomes, and going against the narratives of the powerful.

Moral distinction

A deep problematic issue arises, here: equality of opportunity needs to be defended because it is always being undermined, but meritocracy does not nurture the selfless minds that would be best equipped for the task. So standing up for equality tends to become a moral merit or a status symbol, as well as being necessary to keep society from 'rotting or exploding' from the pressure of 'dreams deferred' as Langston Hughes put it.[81] Paradoxically, by standing up for equality more resolutely than others, individuals can prove themselves greater than others in moral character and therefore status.

It seems something has been lost in this cycle of status-seeking, now that contempt fills the internet, and the lives of those who oppose equality, who are outwardly racist, are proudly stripped of their inherent value. I remember watching the movie *Django Unchained*, about a former slave who kills his former captors in a gruesome manner; listening to the lusty crowd cheer the death of slaveholders, and feeling the invitation to indulge in the cheap elevation of dehumanising the dehumanisers, I felt extraordinarily empty, as did my girlfriend at the time, who was black, and our conversations afterwards set me reflecting more deeply on the subjects in this chapter.

The chorus of people who distinguish themselves by hating and shaming equality's enemies will guard the idea that their behaviour is a source of merit just as closely as the rich guard the image of their own merits. Of course, standing up for equality *is* a source of merit but most powerfully so when it works. It works less well when it is driven by a sense of moral superiority, which tends to create dehumanisation, and thus bitterness and conflict.[82]

Relationship psychologists say that disdain is the single greatest predictor of relationship failure,[83] and that the state of today's politics could be predicted from the tone of yesterday's moral achievement. You can say to a person, 'no, not that way', in a way that will get them to reconsider their actions, or in a way that will ensure they will keep on doing things exactly like they did before, because the tone of your voice tells them whether your request to change their ways is also a request to admit your superiority. If true moral merit is embodied by seeing everybody as sacred we know what tone is needed.

Unearned privilege as sin, and oppression as status in a meritocracy

What a person's group identity means for how their merits have been distorted by historical injustice, and how this must be rectified, forms an endless debate.

One thing that seems certain is that inherited wealth leads, on average, to outcomes that are greater than one's merits. Of course, generalisations are imperfect here, as anywhere. The rich can have struggles with mental illness and family problems that are not obvious. But the rich are not in need of protection, it is assumed, and their privilege has become an easy target. Similar logic has lately been applied to white men more generally. What is important here is that by treating privilege as a sin we hope to bring equality by guilt and shame, and by calling out that sin, people can ostentatiously serve equality. And by agreeing with the callout, one can enter into a certain class of guardians. And soon, pride in the ability to claim moral merit by these displays becomes a sort of class interest, which will be protected just like any source of pleasure.

Mirroring the calculations above regarding privilege, when a person who comes from a background that provided fewer opportunities and more hardship, this means they have greater merits than their outcomes show. Thus oppression is concealed merit, and conveys a form of status. Further, recognising this true status is also a way of righting historical wrongs and an opportunity to prove one's own moral status as rectifier of inequalities, and of claiming membership in the moral elite.

The awkward issue of talent in meritocratic egalitarianism

If the claim that we all get what we want was true, that would be convenient. It would help resolve the tensions inherent in meritocracy's attempts to harness, for the greater good, the part of creative output that is driven by our grasping egos, which have little interest in the greater good, but rather in their own gratification. The system might create general happiness if we all were totally egotistical but equally able to gain rewards and show our merits.

But really, we know that people would be unequal in the things that they can obtain, even if all family connections, political power and inherited wealth were done away with, because of inequality in talents. So, we're faced with a contradiction between, on the one hand, our culture's actual deep tendencies to evaluate people based on achievement and possessions; and on the other hand, our conviction that everybody's life is equally sacred. *Though we often say that 'everybody is equal', we know that it won't end up being the case that everybody has an equal chance at the kind of life that we are all taught to value, and we deal with this largely by just not talking about it.*

The rule seems to be that we deny differences in valuable abilities (talent) except when glaringly obvious perceptual facts or necessities of life force us to admit their existence.[84] For example, we can't deny the existence of size and its importance for some sports. But there is greater denial around more intangible talents such as differences in intelligence and emotional sensitivity. These are often denied, and dwelling on them is resisted with an attitude that is unpleasant enough to get people to change the subject.

Still, we all grow up in classes where some kids are much better than others at sports, and some are much faster or better at answering the hard questions, and we find that almost all important production requires that we use these talents. So we emphasise and subsidise the training of talented scholars and athletes at the same time as we avoid discussing differences in talent.

If we actually discuss the awkward issue of talent out loud, usually somebody will try to diminish this awareness by saying something like, 'being less talented and sexy just means that you need to work harder'. But one cannot wipe out the effects of talent with hard work, because people with talent can also work hard. Another attempt to resolve the problem of talent is to insist that, overall, one person's set of valuable talents must somehow be equal to another's (so the smart *must be* socially awkward, and the athletic *must be* stupid, etc.). No such thing has ever been shown. A variation of this sort of denial is the quasi-religious belief that 'everybody can learn and do whatever they want if they set their mind to it'. This is obviously not true, yet it is often said, even by people with very keen minds. When intelligent people say silly things, it is almost always a sign that hardened ideology is casting a shadow.

It is easy to understand why we try to resist the idea of talent. Talents have been used to justify atrocities. For example, the method by which racists and sexists have justified oppression is by claiming that people's lives are equally sacred, but that oppressed races were unequal in talents and so should not be allowed to run their own lives (like children). It is exactly this stubborn and cruel creativity in justifying oppressive behaviour that has seemed to demonstrate how relying on deep equality alone cannot ensure progress. Egos will find a way to twist the facts in their favour. Something else, which would allow less flexibility and subjectivity in creating excuses, is needed.

Political correctness as an attempt to safeguard and ensure equality

Political correctness is less about attempting to justify equality rationally, and more of a nod to the reality that we cannot defeat all of the ways that people will invent to justify inequality. The extreme on-the-street PC solution, endorsed officially nowhere, but guided by ideology, is to stop the general populace from talking about oppressed groups at all.

The primary target of PC is racism. 'Modern' racism started as an elaborate justification that was needed to get around the moral rules of the day, honed by people who wanted to both claim to be enlightened and to have empires and slaves. Without racism, slaveholders and colonisers would have had to think very badly of themselves. Eventually, racist ideologies fell out of favour 'officially' after their falseness and their perverse and inhuman consequences became too visible to ignore. Of course, it also helped when economic incentives to maintain them changed (e.g. employers simply want the most talented workers). However, to rob others of their humanity while simultaneously proclaiming a stand for equality and freedom requires a major ideologically driven distortion of reality. That is, at least, if one is to avoid being perpetually tortured by one's conscience. Privileged whites have still not looked into the depths of their inherited conditioning, because it would challenge their inherited pride the same way it challenged the pride of the forebears of white identity.

The disruption of this conditioning started a long time ago: the appearance of educated and erudite freed slaves such as Frederick Douglass made the lies on which slavery was built too glaringly obvious to maintain. The uprooting was furthered in the aftermath of the depravities of Nazi Germany where racist ideas were taken to their most extreme form. Further challenges came from civil rights and independence campaigns when murder and abuse were seen alongside extraordinary and inspiring leadership by people of colour. Still the majority of white people merely disbelieve in racist ideas, and disavow the feelings that accompany them, while carrying racist associations.

After civil rights successes, a social consensus of dogmatic racism has been replaced by another, gentler, and preferable dogma, one which sees it as backward (politically incorrect or 'not PC') to discuss differences between groups on any dimension, other than the historical mistreatment or privilege that explains historical inequality. In practice, this is of course impossible; we cannot talk about eight billion humans without generalising, yet we still argue that 'generalisation is impossible'. But this argument is only made when somebody attempts to make a generalisation about a protected group. This leads to countless absurdities and condescensions that help create the caricature of the liberal left that so many love to despise, not least Trump supporters and Fox News viewers. I argue that this dogma also obstructs the as yet incomplete uprooting of racism; instead, it is rather like placing a rock over the roots of a weed. The weed is simply left in the dark, and may someday grow its way out into the open.

We seem to have collectively decided that if we admit that generalisations about groups are sometimes true, we open the door to negative generalisations (assertions of inequality), so we must deny that there are any differences at all (so we are all equal in talents and character). If we are equal in talents and character then all differences in outcome *must* be due to differences in opportunity, and all the space required for resourceful racist impulses to justify themselves is eliminated. So, suggesting that black Americans generally speak with a different accent than white Americans, for example, is a taboo behaviour. Even the importance of culture in political and economic systems has become largely taboo to discuss except for comedians like Dave Chapelle, George Carlin or Triumph the Insult Comic Dog.[85,86,87]

l will give a short example of a conversation that some readers would recognise. I'd like to note before doing this, that I do not mean to single out gay people for discussion, and will admit that this is a bit uncomfortable for me. *However, it really isn't possible to illustrate the overall point without using the example of a specific group that has been historically stigmatised and is therefore now protected by PC norms.*

Virginia: Did you speak to Skyler?

Stacey: No, she wasn't there, a gay man answered the phone, but I don't know him.

Virginia: If you don't know him, how do you know he was gay?

Stacey: He had a gay voice.

Virginia: What is a 'gay voice'?

Stacey: One that sounds like this (*imitating a voice similar to RuPaul Charles*).

Virginia: Oh my god, I'm so ashamed to be related to you.

Stacey: You're so full of it!

Conversations like this happen, and can sometimes strike people as absurd, because it seems like objections are being made to the idea that there is such a thing as a gay accent that would not be made in other cases. For example, nobody would deny that there is such a thing as 'a New York accent', so why the objection to the idea of a 'gay accent'? This is why I have to use examples like 'gay voices' ('black voices' would work just as well), because there are few words that I could substitute for gay and still have a conversation that sounds at all familiar.

I must also note that there are many politically correct liberals who would not raise the objection in the example dialogue, because it is so obvious that there are qualities of a voice that might strongly signal that a person is gay (or black). At the same time, the conversation is an extreme example of a widespread tendency among very liberal people who have spent a good deal of time in the university system where ideals of equality are especially strong.

So, why is there a problem with the idea of a gay voice, or a 'black accent'? I find it useful to break down discomfort with generalisations into three distinct tendencies: 1) the concern that if we condone generalisation, particular people will be burdened with expectations that do not fit them (be stereotyped), for example when somebody is surprised that a gay person does not 'sound gay'; 2) the wish to stop generalisations about groups from being used to justify treating those groups unjustly (unfair discrimination, in other words); 3) relatedly, a strategy to stop discrimination that involves denying generalisations about groups as a whole because we fear those generalisations might be used to justify awful treatment of a group.

Although stereotyping is a real source of harm, I don't think concern over this is mainly what drives people who make the sort of objection that Virginia does in the above example. If we really were concerned simply with the inaccuracy of generalisations, we would actually object to every generalisation. Yet there would be no ring of familiarity in the above conversation if words like 'New Yorker', 'Chicagoan' or 'French' were substituted for 'gay'. We would not object to *those generalisations*. For example, there are quite a lot of people (probably a majority) from Chicago, my home town, who do not speak with an easily recognisable Chicago accent (including me), but they all know what others mean by a Chicago accent and don't take offence at the idea that there is such a thing. Likewise, anybody who knows quite a few gay people knows that there are plenty of gay people who do not 'sound gay' in the way that RuPaul Charles does. But the inaccuracy of Stacey's generalisation is no greater than many other generalisations that we are comfortable with.

It is also hard to believe that Virginia is driven by a concern that a straight person is being mistaken for gay. We might think that she is worried that the gay people who don't sound gay are being unfairly stereotyped. Of course they really aren't in this case: the person who answered the phone is just being assumed to be gay, and there is nothing wrong with being gay (and I assume Virginia would agree). If she (or we) were generally concerned about people being put in boxes that they don't belong in, we would especially be concerned with stereotypes such as that Irish/Russians/Australians drink too much or Germans are humourless racists. We are not very concerned at all with *these* generalisations because they are not perceived as providing the raw materials for a systematic attempt to justify inequality.

Mostly, we hear it said that 'you can't generalise' when somebody makes generalisations about stigmatised groups because these historically oppressed groups have an ideological protection from being generalised about at all. The most notable example is women. We wouldn't expect to hear an objection by Virginia if Stacey said, 'a woman answered the phone' (though this may happen in the most liberal circles), because it just can't be denied that women's voices are usually different from men's. Generalisations about male and female voices are still politically correct because it would be so hard to live without them. However, you will hear resistance, in certain sectors of society, to all sorts of generalisations about women (that they are shorter and less physically strong than men, spend more money on make-up, like shopping, are generally better cooks than men, are more interested in people, more drawn to children and so on). It is very important to some guardians of equality to correct people when they make these generalisations, and to prove that all but the physical (obviously true) differences are due to unequal treatment in the social environment – though many of these generalisations are statistically true and seem rooted in biology. Research finds both strong effects of socialisation *and* strong innate differences between sexes.

The emergent cultural programme known as 'the PC movement' is driven by impulses to short-circuit institutional oppression, which has a certain kind of nobility to it, but it also has a dishonesty and hubris. These efforts are generally hubristic because these conversations are often transparently driven by the desire for status on the part of the person objecting (which has become the basis of 'call out' culture). We are all vain (including me). People make these objections more out of an understandable desire to be morally superior to others than to protect an oppressed group. This conversation is dishonest because it attempts to ban generalisations about stigmatised groups by claiming that generalisations aren't possible, when obviously *little is possible in life without generalisations*. It is transparent that these objections are about setting bounds on *what types of generalisations* can be made *by whom*.

This absurd, selective pretence that generalisations are generally undesirable amounts to a decision by one class of people (educated and liberal) about what types of generalisations can be entertained by whom. Of course nobody can avoid committing the invented sin of generalisation with every sentence. Prohibiting discussions by invoking reasons that are obviously not true is basically a display of authority. It is the ability to get away with this that marks the PC crowd out as 'elites'. So, while proceeding under the mantle of egalitarian truth-seeking, this performance of egalitarianism is dogmatic and status driven.

The excesses of PC culture have few serious opponents among those who support the aim of equality. PC is ugly, we say to ourselves, but it is all for the best: after all, a politically correct ban on generalisation will stop people from dreaming up elaborate new justifications for why some people have so much more than others. Or so we hope.

Of course, the election of Donald Trump and a host of nationalist leaders was the nature of reality showing through. It reveals what many expected but could not prove. Political correctness has not done away with racism, but only made it taboo to express. At the same time, the liberal elite, which is virtually identified by its use of PC rhetoric, which includes disdain, is Trump's favourite target. Jordan Peterson became internationally famous, initially, for mounting credible defences of a few non-PC claims, such as that, as a group, women show less interest in science and technology jobs. The overstep in power represented by the above-discussed dynamics is becoming a liability to the project of treating all people in a way that is consistent with universal love.

Power, nationalism and tribalism
in the shadow of equality

At this point I feel prepared to remark further on the shadow that equality casts on power, imperialism and colonialism. By power, I mean here an ability to get others to do what one desires, rather than the 'inner power' of spiritual freedom.[88] Power over others is something that humans are inherently capable of desiring, but which is by nature scarce, obtained by many only in worlds of fantasy and video games. As mentioned, the possession of power is inherently in conflict with either deep or surface equality so it is mostly taboo to express, pursue or claim. Still, it determines many social dynamics.

Power advantages are often not openly expressed, such as in workplaces, where bosses do not present themselves as bosses,[89] or in imperial wars that are discussed as exercises in liberation. Power disadvantage is also uncomfortable to admit because it can offend one's self-image as an equal. That is, until public morality shifts so that, by discussing unequal power, people can use moral force to challenge it. Discussions of sexual harassment, micro-aggressions and patriarchal behaviour have built this kind of moral force in recent times.

If the discussions that take place after these ideas hit the mainstream are sometimes a little clumsy and imprecise, part of the reason for this, I would suggest, is that we have discussed the reality of the drive to power so little. So when these subjects, which are all about power, do come up, they come up in a vacuum of discussion. Again the question arises: are we well served by taboos and dogmas against behaviours and drives that conflict with equality? Rather, I contend, we can compassionately accept that the drive for power exists *and* is very often a cause of suffering. Dropping taboos on discussing sex, mental illness and same-sex attraction are all positive developments, and open discussion of power would also be helpful. We might protest that admitting power gives us an image of humans that is out of line with our pursuit of justice, but that is the point. Humans are the way they are, no matter how we think of them. We have to engage with the realities of power in order to construct a culture that can deal with power effectively.

The taboo on accepting the drive to power may explain why Europe's colonial history and America's current unacknowledged empire are also badly understood. The drive for collective experience of power and glory is, as much as anything, what drove Europeans to fight for 'their place in the Sun' through empire-building,[90] and it also underlies domestic support of US military adventurism. A society in which citizens are demanding to be equal or close to equal to their leaders can still satisfy citizens' drive for power – by dominating people outside that society. This powerful drive only relented among Europe's great states after the pursuit of national glory erupted into two empire-shattering worldwide wars that claimed tens of millions of lives and resulted in atrocities so ghastly that they forced Europe to question its claims to civilisation. It was largely an extreme experience of the maniacal pursuit of national superiority that convinced us that equality is *the truth*. But our dogmatic way of pursuing equality is sowing confusion by limiting what can be said. Ill-effects cannot be fathomed by people who think they are standing for good. Fruitful dialogue on these points will be hard, but can be helped along by seeing the grand sweep of history that we are caught in more fully.[91]

4 Doing Something

Intellectual works are necessary but convince few

I HAVE TRIED to write a scientifically consistent but still lifelike story about our history, to suggest ways of understanding our times that are useful, embodied and lifelike. The story revolves around our collective cultivation of several related attachments that have become counterproductive because of their strength. I've pointed out that these views reflect a move away from spirituality and related ways of being (sisterly and brotherly love), and have drawn on Zen Buddhism to suggest other ways of looking at the world that could usefully transform this way of being.

However, I certainly don't think this book, or any book, will change the world much, just by itself. The reality is that our attachment to rationality and believing in beliefs lead us to overrate the importance of written works, even those much better and longer than this one. Many more notable people than me have said that our analytical focus has resulted in strange relations to ourselves, each other and nature.

Siddhartha Gautama (aka 'the Buddha') taught 2,500 years ago that the closest connection to truth is not intellectual, but rather comes when we learn to live peacefully in the present moment. Virtually everyone has heard of his work, but the words haven't persuaded us deeply.

Nietzsche argued that the Dionysian intelligence, related to the idea of guidance discussed here, was a superior form of understanding that the West was losing. Perhaps the message didn't get through so much because he paired it with strange-sounding notions of the Ubermensch.

Martin Heidegger, one of the 20th century's most influential philosophers, wrote that our intellectual approach to being was impairing our living of life itself. He urged 'being in the world' – returning to the present moment – and went on to state that our over-reliance on intellect caused us to view nature as a great 'filling station' (gas station). One could argue that he is hard to read (correctly) and then conclude this is why his ideas haven't been sufficiently influential (erroneously).

Joanna Macy writes accessibly, and connects our environmental crisis to our feeling of separation from nature and loss of connection to unity that comes in mystical states. She also relies on Buddhist worldviews to argue for a programme of reconnection. Maybe she has been too easily dismissed as a hippie and her work is not read enough.

Iain McGilchrist has more recently written about the connections between the sort of intelligence that underlies guidance and the right hemisphere of the brain. He argued that Western civilisation has disappeared into the left hemisphere's world of abstractions, with consequences that are bound to be disastrous. Perhaps his voice has just been muted because of a historical accident whereby popular myths about the hemispheres have made any discussion of the right and left hemispheres seem ridiculous.

More likely, however, is that the notions these people put forward, and the distinction between the forms of intelligence that all of these authors are gesturing at, are simply very difficult to grasp, and this is part of the human condition that makes self-understanding so elusive. We can understand ourselves best when we explore both the use of intellect and of guidance, but this is really, really hard. Creating conditions for this exploration will do more to further the different understanding than additional books will. There's nothing wrong with writing, but being attached to the power of writing to bring understanding is unhealthy.

A community of thought and consciousness

Creating communities and spaces where people can remain aware of cultural shadows, if not free from them, is part of allowing the emergence of new ways of seeing and acting. The simple practice of sharing space and commitments helps us to see the limits of an individualist mindset. Simply being around others who are aware of the story of progress, based in rationality, individuality and equality, is just a way of seeing things, and helps us all to become less identified with this story. The transformation required is large and multifaceted, but the awareness at the heart of it can be cultivated.

The human mind can be said to be 'a bag of habits'. The shadows detailed earlier in this book arise from habits of perception and thought that are communicated culturally. Disabusing ourselves of these habits is not something that is best done by simply adopting new beliefs. We can create a new milieu.

Basically, we might say we are addicted to the ways of thinking described above: to rationality, to individuality, to equality. Addictions are simply compulsive habits that we or others recognise as undesirable, but that we are unable to rid ourselves of. They are patterns of behaviour that are driven by craving certain sensations, where we have come to recognise that those behaviours have negative consequences, *and* despite this awareness, our cravings are too strong to resist and we continue those behaviours. We may admit that attachment to our ways of thinking are problematic, but they are what we use to navigate life and get what we want.

The first rule of changing bad habits (such as drug addiction) of all kinds is to limit your exposure to people who have the same (bad) habits of thought and behaviour and to surround oneself with others who have good habits of thought and behaviour. This is hard in a society of people who believe the same things. That is why monasteries, isolated from the world, have been the preferred place to relieve oneself of the addiction to the view that we are the centre of the world, and why rehab centres and support groups enable people to get off drugs.

Individuals cannot respond to the situation alone. Independence is a mere abstraction and we should start acting like it. Life Itself is part of a movement towards creating the spaces where people can collectively change their habitual patterns of being, perceiving and acting. In hubs in major cities and in the countryside, we seek to create spaces where people can explore different ways of being together while still remaining engaged with society so that we can bring the awareness we cultivate to our most pressing challenges.

Is this just another 'echo chamber'? At the risk of being blithe, I'll note that the pejorative against echo travels most strongly within a liberal educated community that is a bit of an echo chamber itself. People outside that echo chamber realise that communication requires some level of shared perspective and culture. The difference between a community with a shared culture and an echo chamber has to do with whether there is an ability to listen to the outside world. A community will always have more contact among themselves than they do with those outside of the community – if not, they would not be a community. And people will always form communities with like-minded others. But that does not mean they are cut off from others.[92]

Notions always reach their greatest fulfilment when they are pursued together by a community, whether scientific notions pursued within the scientific community, artistic notions pursued within artists' movements, or spiritual notions pursued within churches, monasteries and ashrams. The more radically different the notion to be explored, the more likely the people who hold it seek contact with others who share the same notion (again, think recovering drug addicts).

Exploring the false alternative between intellectual rigour and being in the moment is a radical pursuit. The overemphasis on rationality has created reactions against rationality and logic in some corners of society, so that spiritual spheres and intellectual spheres are seen as almost in opposition to each other. This would be a grave mistake. Reason is not rationality; spirituality is not new-ageism.

There is a lot to gain from forming such a community of practice and thought. Activism that can guide us skilfully through the complex mess we are in requires the ability to remain in touch with our guidance, but also logistics and organisation. Though 'just let it flow' is an attractive sentiment, anybody who actually organises the retreats and festivals where counterculture is strong knows that a lot of planning is necessary to create the conditions where people can flow. What we are looking to do is create situations where people can live this way while remaining in touch with (currently) conventional society.

A monastery is one example of an organised community that creates the conditions for presence. A monastery is not a perfect model for what must be achieved, but there is real overlap, such as shared community practices that help us get in touch with ourselves and each other. Smaller communities which are not organised along monastic lines also frequently have shared practices. Some of these might be labelled religious within Western traditional ways of thinking, but the mindfulness movement has done a good job of showing that we can engage in shared practice not out of habitual religiosity, but a need for sanity.

Firstly, in order to be economically viable and engaged, it is useful to have access to urban centres, and, in order to be culturally viable (and visible), it is useful to have plenty of shared space. These two needs are in conflict. What is necessary is a system of spaces that allows people to spend time in the cities and also in the countryside closer to nature and beauty and where it is easier to create a space where we live together. We find that there are an increasing number of people who are committing themselves to the pursuit of honouring both guidance and rigour and think that group is at the requisite number in order to form such spaces.

Awareness

More important than reflection at this point is organising for awareness. Again, the Buddhist Sangha can form something of an inspiration here. The Sangha essentially is a group of people who practise together to transform their collective and personal mindset, consciousnesses and ways of being. Sanghas are generally open to all people. The basic movement of a practitioner can be described as moving from vaguely and shallowly understanding intellectual notions, such as embracing awareness of our suffering, releasing attachment and accepting impermanence, to true insight into these so that our thoughts and actions reflect this awareness effortlessly: starting out as people who say every moment could be our last and becoming people who know this as deeply as possible.

We do not have to totally master these ancient spiritual truths to increase our chances of navigating to a better future. There is a lot of abstract understanding that our society is unsustainable, that our continued attachment to material gain is obsolete, and that we face huge challenges in finding a way forward. We cannot address our social situation without transforming the abstract understanding of these into deeper awareness. Wisdom traditions, and modern innovations such as 12-step programmes,can help us do this.[93]

The gravity of our collective dysfunction relative to our individual ability to address this is enormous. It is easy to just turn away from the big picture we are presented with. As with personal awareness, we often remain unaware of our collective situation because of what we would have to acknowledge and give up if we saw the big picture. Our jobs and accomplishments seem less important in the face of personal mortality. The difficulty of being aware of our personal smallness and mortality has traditionally been addressed in groups. The difficulty of the current social task and the vastness of the opportunity must also be understood as a group.

Mindful enquiry into morality, values and purpose

A paramount challenge of our times is to achieve clear values, views and priorities that can serve as the foundation for collective flourishing. Fuller and richer insights are needed, and are more than logic alone can provide. They will come from 'mindful enquiry' and deep reflection, with a held awareness of what ideas imply for our daily existence. The popularisation of mindfulness practice has given many of us a way to touch embodied understanding, and a chance for many of us to shift deep convictions as well as intellectual positions, and to get in greater touch with 'life itself', which is the basis of all value. A popular course along these lines has always been desirable, and, with increasing interest in big questions, and openness to contemplation, this is now possible. We are exploring how to use guided but open enquiry, grounded in a mindful approach, to bring together both age-old and brand-new reflective exercises that consider questions in quantum physics, phenomenology, and Greek and Buddhist traditions of enquiry (among others), all with the aim of deepening participants' insight into the human condition.

Devoted mindful enquiry is about true insight, such as into our own impermanence, or moving from simply agreeing that we are all interdependent to accepting this 'in our bones'. Deep reflection and centred awareness of our feelings can allow us to explore and accept these truths.

The identification and refinement of course content will form the basis of the project. Early ideas include:

- Are success and money the highest goals, or can we be happy with simplicity?

- What are the limits to reason, and the consequences of desiring certainty? Quantum physics has shown the entanglement of all things – defying our intuitions. Reflection on this can make it clear that our ability to analyse and separate is simply a tool (a useful one, but limited).

• Enquiring into the limits of language using both contemporary linguistics and ancient reflections.

• Considering the constructed nature of concepts and objects.

• Enquiry into the interconnected nature of things through diverse paradigms, from systems theory to the ancient Chinese 'harmonic web of life'.

• Reflecting on the concept of individuality and the construction of the self concept.

• Are mind and body separate?

• How do I and could I relate to other people and the planet? Reflection on moral rules versus moral intuitions and potential for contemplation to develop one's own ethical basis for life.

Such questions have engaged thinkers and contemplatives through the ages, and there are many different answers. Generally, whichever answer one ends up with, one will live a saner life by having deeply examined these questions, especially in light of scientific evidence. Mindful enquiry has been known to raise awareness of interconnectedness and humility regarding the limits of knowledge. Awareness of interconnection is especially influential in moral issues where self and community interests must be balanced.

It is often noted, however, that mindfulness programmes are divorced from the intellectual and moral context of the Buddhist tradition. The sensitivity, openness and care cultivated through mindfulness training can help moral change when paired with explicit consideration of underpinning philosophical views. However, rather than following a traditional Buddhist framework, it may be most broadly effective in the

Western context if mindfulness is used to complement the existing cultural emphasis on free enquiry.

Contemplative citizen neuroscience

Despite the headlines generated by contemplative neuroscience, the core contentions of contemplative traditions have only just been touched upon by science. Examples include the distinction between attachment, detachment and non-attachment, and the question of what is meant by 'choiceless choice'. These are all crucial to the Buddhist tradition's central goal of alleviating suffering but have received little attention. The disconnect arises partly from difficulty in studying inner life, and partly from unaligned incentives and perspectives of contemplative practitioners, scholars and scientists. Collaboration is impeded by distances between a conceptual understanding of Buddhist tradition and 'true insight' coming from practice, between effectively demonstrating the Dharma (Buddhists' typical goal), and getting publications in prestigious journals (especially important for scientists relying on expensive fMRI methods).

We propose to address this situation by creating a conduit through which 'the contemplative community' can encourage studies that reflect their understanding and experience of the mind and the possibilities for a cessation of suffering.[94] Organisations that provide a partial model for this effort are scientifically active membership organisations for those with neural atypicalities such as autism spectrum disorder. Groups of this type have successfully redirected study of their condition using insights derived from a lived experience that scientists typically cannot share, and they raise money on an ongoing basis. In the proposed body, senior practitioners, chosen by their peers for their ability to engage with science and advised by scientists and Buddhist scholars, would recommend the scientific study of propositions derived from core Buddhist notions, and help guide their translation into neuroscientifically testable propositions. The structure of this body would itself be the subject of consultations with contemplatives, scientists and experts in organisational structure.

Of course, contemplatives are set apart from patient groups in that their states result from a discipline that is as old as philosophy, literature or mathematics. It has at least an equal tradition of dedication and sees itself as the most potent means of self-understanding and radical well-being. Scientists would be most successfully engaged if willing to consider interdisciplinary perspectives on truth, perhaps even to the point of practising themselves. Strict adherence to open science would be important to counter (quite reasonable) suspicions that such practices would skew findings.

5 Contemplative Activism

EVERYTHING THAT Life Itself aspires to, including even community building, could fall under the banner of 'contemplative activism'. Broadly, this means a few things: acting from a perspective grounded in contemplation, which involves knowing ourselves and life through direct observation, in order to create better conditions for human flourishing. Right now we might identify climate change as a clear and present danger, but, as mentioned, we believe that our CO_2 problem is rooted in our ways of being. We must see the whole problem clearly to get anywhere with it.

Being contemplative does not mean that we don't reason or use logic. Rather, contemplation leads us to appreciate that thoughts have effects which can be useful. We aspire to develop and maintain the awareness that we are more than our thoughts. That our thoughts are tools, while our being, life itself, is the most important thing. But we can use the intellect in service of this most important thing, and in fact we must, if we are to protect what is most important.

Noticing this, we can respond to an objection to the idea of activism from a contemplative perspective. There is a misconception that contemplatives don't try to change things. Of course this isn't true. All of the most famous contemplatives spent their lives teaching, helping others to suffer less. Teachers can be seen as changing minds, and ultimately every social change is about changing minds. We say things like *teachers don't teach, students learn*, but this is just our individualist conceptions of independence speaking – obviously both matter. If every thinker and mystic had put their notes in the fireplace and refused students, we obviously would not have developed either technical or spiritual traditions.

Activism is about changing minds and ways of being. It is both similar to and different from teaching. The most notable difference is that the minds we seek to influence may not volunteer their participation. In fact, they may even be actively opposed – think of Gandhi working for an independent India or King for a fair America. Activism implies confrontation and vigorously disrupting the awareness and behaviours of others. Protests, rallies and civic disobedience – even lobbying – are all ways to grab the attention of others, rather than, as a teacher does, directing attention that is freely given. Activism also means organising among activists to confront societies with what they do not see and perhaps do not want to see.

The task of activists who would like to deal with the kind of awareness that is gestured towards in this book is really to get people to see that their own best available alternative is something very different from what they suppose – and even beyond what they can actually conceive. This is because what we conceive is formed within the confines of our fundamental assumptions and views, about reality and ourselves – views that we take for the truth but which are, in fact, very different from the truth.

Some readers may notice that they feel this sounds arrogant or superior to them. Unfortunately, sounding so is inevitable when one says the world is very wrong about something very important – at least in our current way of perceiving things, which mandates that we must be sure to 'be equal' at all times. There are many people who understand at an intuitive level what has been written in this book. Typically, they have different practices and different vocabularies that could be more than the sum of their parts. Contemplative activism is about working to make this happen.

Sustainable well-being and returning to life itself

In dealing with the climate crisis, the most important immediate task may be to convert our belief that 'the best things in life are free' into a conviction. If this sounds too much like relying on folksy wisdom, we can talk in terms of psychology.

It has long been known that a lack of personal connection, food and shelter makes it difficult to develop as a person, and, furthermore, that when these needs are met we look for meaning, and, finally, self-actualisation. Maslow's famous pyramid, which captures these points, has been in textbooks for generations (though superseded by better models that agree on these main points[95]). Data backs up the idea that our happiness goes up quite a lot as we move from struggling for food and shelter to material security, but beyond this point, material things do much less for us. Yet our societies continue obsessively to prioritise material growth – an obsession at the root of the climate crisis. What we need are better priorities and, more importantly, a movement at the cultural and political levels strong enough to reorientate our lives according to those priorities.

The impetus for this movement may well be the climate change situation. The facts suggest that it is possible to increase what actually really matters, the quality of our conscious experience of life, while massively decreasing our consumption and our carbon emissions. We should have de-emphasised growth in favour of the quality of life itself a long time ago, but we must do this now. Remaining aware of this can make dealing with climate change much less painful.

Pioneers in various fields have been working on this for decades. First psychotherapy, then the mindfulness movement, and now more recent 'embodied' methods for dealing with trauma: somatic experiencing, mindfulness-based therapies, various bodywork methods, Rolfing and so on. These have provided concrete ways for people to go about recovering from trauma and moving towards what used to be called 'self-actualisation'. Fashion may have moved towards calling this 'adult development' if you trust science, or healing and transformation if you prefer ancient wisdom traditions, but the basic facts are stable. Doing something about them is now necessary. Given that something like 20 per cent of the population is traumatised, and these people report especially low life satisfaction and are likely to spread their suffering to family and co-workers, a social policy focusing on trauma could increase societies' life satisfaction more than all of the income gains of the past several decades. To do this, we have to convince ourselves at a deeper level that a lack of money is not the major cause of suffering in our societies.

This is not a question of waiting for more science on the relative importance of money. As with climate change, we have the data we need to agree on a change in general policy direction – towards cultivating well-being with lower environmental impact. Research can continue to amass evidence on particular practices, such as mindfulness, that allow people to be far happier with a few simple lifestyle adjustments, but large-scale healing can begin as soon as there is political will. We need activism, however, that turns the growing direct knowledge that inner work can create greater joy into real political change. There are conversations on social-scale trauma recovery being promoted by people such as Tomas Hübl, and the long-running mindfulness movement.[96] It has not yet got political: rather it has remained in the non-partisan space afforded to 'medical' concerns. A widespread discussion of how to design a society that puts such goals at its centre is necessary, but this will be made possible by allowing greater space in public conversation for personal intuitive experience, which all people must rely on for healing and growth, greater emphasis on collective action and prioritisation of compassionate dialogue over moral superiority.

Endnotes

1   Utopian visions have been unfairly maligned because visions of the recent past have lacked humility and reflected exactly the cultural habits that I discuss in this book. For a defence of Utopianism see: Rufus Pollock's short essay, https://artearthtech.com/2017/10/20/pragmatic-utopians/.

2   The works of Thich Nhat Hanh, Iain McGilchrist, Joanna Macy and Martin Heidegger, for example, are all quite well known and I am indebted to all of them.

3   Albert Einstein, *Out of My Later Years*, Wings Books, New York, 1996.

4   Karl Marx and Friedrich Engels, *The Communist Manifesto*, W.W. Norton, 1848.

5   Thomas Armstrong, *7 Kinds of Smart: Identifying and Developing Your Multiple Intelligences*, Plume, 2001

6   J. Krishnamurti, *Education and the Significance of Life*, Harper & Row, 1981

7   Feynman Lectures on Physics, No. 8 Motion, https://www.feynmanlectures.caltech.edu/I_08.html

8   Even there, we'd get into problems if we questioned our definitions too much. When atoms change, such as during fusion, there must be a point at which there are still two atoms and a point at which they become one atom – when, precisely, is that point? I am not suggesting that 'we don't even know what an atom is', but our knowledge is still imprecise.

9   A cornerstone of the 'laissez-faire' capitalist view that ruthless competition creates the best of all possible worlds was taken from Adam Smith, who famously said in *The Wealth of Nations* (1776) that self-interested businessmen, by inventing ruthlessly efficient business practices, often increased the public's wealth 'as if guided by an invisible hand'. But this cornerstone has had to be removed from the house that Smith himself was building with his writings, in order to be used in the ideological fortresses of extreme capitalism. Smith's own purpose with such statements was limited to illustrating that selfishly motivated capitalists are driven towards efficient use of materials and workers' time. The great wealth produced by markets and capitalism was lifting many people out of material poverty. Smith also wrote about the terrible effects of factory work on workers and against many imperial policies. And he wrote: 'If we saw ourselves in the light in which others see us, or in which they would see us if they knew all, a reformation would generally be unavoidable. We could not otherwise endure the sight.' He would not be surprised that his ideas have been abused.

10 https://www.nytimes.com/2019/08/08/climate/climate-change-food-supply.html

11 See: https://www.esquire.com/news-politics/a36228/ballad-of-the-sad-climatologists-0815/

12 Certain environmental groups, such as the Transition town movement, might be an exception. Climate science might also be thought to be an exception, but actually the International Panel on Climate Change (IPCC) has been consistently optimistic; this has been empirically shown, and publicly admitted by leading members of that body. See: https://www.skepticalscience.com/ipcc-scientific-consensus.htm

13 See: https://www.ipcc.ch/sr15/

14 Ibid.

15 For a longer exploration of this point see: https://artearthtech.com/2020/03/25/letting-go-of-being-enlightened/ .

16 I won't try, though, because actually the rise of nationalism is quite complicated. The story includes privilege and factors discussed later on in this work.

17 https://www.nber.org/papers/w18992.pdf

18 Wolfers and Stevenson commonly plot their data by putting income on a logarithmic scale which makes the plot into a straight line. This may help to strengthen the impression that their main contention – more income always leads to more happiness – supports a continued focus on economic growth.

19 Questions of addiction are then ultimately based on judgement and can be controversial, because opinions differ on what is clearly detrimental.

20 See: https://rufuspollock.com/2008/11/03/buddhist-economics/

21 De Tocqueville, A. (2003). *Democracy in America* (Vol. 10). Regnery Publishing.

22 There are a number of scientific and intellectual attempts to usher this ability into respectability, which I will discuss in detail as part of the discussion of rationality. For now, I simply ask the reader to note that these have not succeeded in creating a lucid societal understanding of this ability.

23 That is, it will come from god, ancestors, the earth, psychic powers, the universe, the brain, the 'right brain', and so on, depending on the person. These answers about the source of guidance are manifold, and likely come from the intellectual traditions of their culture. While the direction provided, by whatever putative source, is more similar on many questions, such as those of basic morality. There are a great many things about which guidance, unaided by the intellect and science, tells us little

or nothing, I think the ultimate source of guidance is one of these. But this is no reason to ignore guidance.

24 For research and discussion of the deep connection between persuasion and self-deception see: Robert Trivers, https://www.edge.org/conversation/robert_trivers-deceit-and-self-deception

25 See: Hoehl, S., Keupp, S., Schleihauf, H., McGuigan, N., Buttelmann, D., & Whiten, A. (2019). 'Over-imitation': A review and appraisal of a decade of research. *Developmental Review*, 51, 90–108.

26 Readers who feel that I am singling out Catholicism are advised to remember that I am discussing the Catholic Church because it was the dominant wisdom tradition in all of Western Europe, having historically anomalous power, and therefore its excesses are of special historical significance.

27 I apologise here for the sweeping and brief nature of this statement, but I think it is fair, if crude, and a vast amount of facts would have to be introduced to fully discuss the vast and shifting details of the Church's claim on guidance.

28 Indulgences were essentially money payments for the forgiveness of sins that allowed a person to redeem themselves after a scandal.

29 For an account of some of the abuses of this period in a Jesuit (Catholic) periodical, see: Anderson, C. (2005). An 11th-century Scandal. *America Magazine*: https://www.americamagazine.org/issue/534/article/11th-century-scandal

30 Hayek, F (1980). *The Counter-Revolution of Science: Studies on the Abuse of Reason.* Liberty Fund.

31 For insightful discussion see: Gleiser, M. (2014). *The Island of Knowledge: The limits of science and the search for meaning.* Basic Books.

32 For a sceptical review, which nonetheless concludes that mindfulness can be very useful, see: https://www.bbc.com/future/article/20180502-does-mindfulness-really-improve-our-health

33 Hacking, I. & Hacking, J. (1999). *The Social Construction of What?* Harvard University Press.

34 Hoffman, D. (1998). *Visual Intelligence: How we create what we see* (First ed.). New York: W.W. Norton.

35 Siderits, M., Thompson, E. & Zahavi, D. (Eds.). (2011). *Self, No Self?: Perspectives from analytical, phenomenological, and Indian traditions.* Oxford University Press.

36 Ricard, M., Thuan, T. X. & Trinh, X. T. (2001). *The Quantum and the Lotus: A journey to the frontiers where science and Buddhism meet* (No. 151). Broadway Books.

37 For an extended discussion of these points see: Stephen Bachelor's *After Buddhism.*

38 See: Gil Fronsdahl's article: Should I Believe in Rebirth? at: https://tinyurl.com/yyr6qvdg; or Thich Nhat Hanh's discussion of life after death at: https://www.youtube.com/watch?v=QGbVPsc2jIo&t=49s

39 Christopher Frey, Aristotle's Irredeemable Ableism, https://churchlifejournal.nd.edu/articles/aristotles-irredeemable-ableism/

40 Physicists use the word 'energy' very differently, to mean the stuff that makes matter move. It is worth noting that different people use the same word in different ways. The Ancient Greek term from which energy derives was closer to the colloquial usage. I find that 'quality of mind' avoids filling readers' minds with too much of the intellectual 'energy' that is associated with the academic usage of Latin.

41 See the Life Itself white paper on well-being for an exploration of similar dynamics regarding wellness at: https://lifeitself.us/institute/radical-well-being

42 For a seminal discussion, see: Jackson, S.A. & Csikszentmihalyi, M. (1999). *Flow in Sports*. Human Kinetics.

43 See the classic discussion of colour-blind vision scientists in Jackson, F. (1982). Epiphenomenal Qualia. *Philosophical Quarterly*, 32(127), 127–136.

44 Thus the famous quote, attributed to Max Planck, that 'science advances one funeral at a time'.

45 See, for example: Kingsnorth, P. & Hine, D. (2009) Uncivilisation: The Dark Mountain Manifesto https://dark-mountain.net/about/manifesto/

46 e.g. https://www.cnbc.com/2019/03/25/heres-what-warren-buffett-thinks-about-climate-change-and-inve sting.html

47 e.g. https://www.theatlantic.com/magazine/archive/2015/11/we-need-an-energy-miracle/407881/

48 For a particularly good discussion of this see: Jonathan Rowson's respiritualise https://www.systems-souls-society.com/publications.

49 Csikszentmihalyi, M. (1997). *Flow and the Psychology of Discovery and Invention*. HarperPerennial, New York, p. 39.

50 Polanyi, M. (2015). *Personal Knowledge: Towards a post-critical philosophy*. University of Chicago Press.

51 Norenzayan, A., Smith, E.E., Kim, B.J. & Nisbett, R.E. (2002). Cultural Preferences for Formal Versus Intuitive Reasoning. *Cognitive Science*, 26(5), 653–684.

52 Rock, I. & Palmer, S. (1990). The Legacy of Gestalt Psychology. *Scientific American*, 263(6), 84–91.

53 Goleman, D. (2006). *Emotional Intelligence*. Bantam.

54 Dijksterhuis, A. & Strick, M. (2016). A Case for Thinking without Consciousness. *Perspectives on Psychological Science*, 11(1), 117–132.

55 cited in Pugh, G.E. (1977) *The Biological Origin of Human Values*, New York: Basic Books

56 (1962) *Profiles of the Future*, Phoenix

57 (1992) *The Computational Brain*, MIT Press

58 Note that individualism is less a formal political belief and more a description of a tendency that consistently arises in liberal societies. I use individualism here in the popular sense of the term – roughly meaning a worldview in which the individual and their freedom are unquestionably pre-eminent and social institutions are there to protect individuals.

59 For a lucid account of how individualism grew from seeds provided by Christianity see: Siedentop, L. (2014). *Inventing the Individual*. Harvard University Press.

60 Milgram, S. (1965). Some Conditions of Obedience and Disobedience to Authority. *Human Relations*, 18(1), 57-76.

61 Burger, J. (2009). Replicating Milgram: Would people still obey today? *American Psychologist*, 64(1), 1.

62 Miller, J.G. (1984). Culture and the Development of Everyday Social Explanation. *Journal of Personality and Social Psychology*. 46(5), 961–978.

63 Henrich, J., Heine, S.J. and Norenzayan, A. (2010). The Weirdest People in the World? *Behavioral and Brain Sciences*, 33.2, 61–83.

64 Becker, M. et al. (2012). Culture and the Distinctiveness Motive: Constructing identity in individualistic and collectivistic contexts. *Journal of Personality and Social Psychology*, 102.4, 833.

65 Keynes, J.M. (1936) *The General Theory of Employment, Interest and Money*, Macmillan & Co.

66 Kavanagh, L.C. & Winkielman, P. (2016). The Functionality of Spontaneous Mimicry and its Influences on Affiliation: An implicit socialization account. *Frontiers in Psychology*, 7, 458.

67 For an example see: Piers Morgan's criticism of Extinction Rebellion's Skeena Rathore, https://www.youtube.com/watch?v=8ISePLL1wcw

68 Ostrom, E. (2008). The Challenge of Common-pool Resources. *Environment: Science and Policy for Sustainable Development*, 50(4), 8–21.

69 For a nuanced discussion see: Gelin, M. (2018) Silicon Valley's libertarians are trading blows with California Democrats in a fight for the left, Quartz. https://tinyurl.com/y3yvmct2

70 As delivered in many talks (also see https://www.stillwatermpc.org/dharma-topics/content-to-be-simply-myself/)

71 Andrew Serrano's controversial photo of a crucifix suspended in his own urine might become all the more emblematic of a loss of a sensibility of the sacred when we consider that he didn't anticipate controversy. See: https://en.wikipedia.org/wiki/Piss_Christ

72 Every field of social science attests to this, psychology through anthropology, as well as literary classics such as William Golding's *Lord of the Flies*. For a non-fiction review see: Matthew White (2013). *Atrocities: The 100 Deadliest Episodes in Human History*. W.W. Norton.

73 https://kinginstitute.stanford.edu/king-papers/documents/american-dream-sermon-delivered-ebenezer-baptist-church

74 Merton, T. (2009). *Conjectures of a Guilty Bystander*. Image.

75 For further discussion of these categories and evidence about whether meritocracy is practically achieved see: McNamee, S.J. & Miller, R.K. (2009). *The Meritocracy Myth*. Rowman & Littlefield.

76 Although capitalist ideology helps to reinforce this idea, this idea helps ideology deeply.

77 It is useful to think of the request 'don't think of a pink elephant' here (following George Lakoff) the net effect of which is to make us think of nothing but pink elephants.

78 The Combahee River Collective, (1977) The Combahee River Collective Statement. See: https://www.blackpast.org/african-american-history/combahee-river-collective-statement-1977/

79 For an extended discussion of this dynamic and how it creates anxiety about accomplishments, see: de Botton, A. (2008). *Status Anxiety*. Vintage.

80 See again McNamee & Miller for discussion of the mythologising of meritocracy.

81 'Montage of a Dream Deferred', In: Rampersad, Arnold. *The Collected Poems of Langston Hughes*. New York: Alfred A. Knopf; 1995. p. 387. Online at: https://www.poetryfoundation.org/poems/46548/harlem

82 This pattern of behaviour is known, in some circles, as the 'mean green meme', a term owed to Ken Wilber, who discussed it in the context of his Integral Theory in his 2001 book: *A Theory of Everything: An integral vision for business, politics, science and spirituality*. Shambhala Publications.

83 See, for example, Gottman, J.M. (2008). Gottman Method Couple Therapy. *Clinical Handbook of Couple Therapy*, 4(8), 138–164.

84 Note that it is meaningful talent we worry about; it is not necessary to avoid talking about an ability to roll the tongue or double-jointedness because these offend nobody's sense of self-worth.

85 e.g. Sticks and Stones https://en.wikipedia.org/wiki/Sticks_%26_Stones_(film)

86 e.g. https://www.youtube.com/watch?v=G9n8Xp8DWf8

87 e.g. Triumph the Insult Comic Dog Talks to Young Voters: https://www.youtube.com/watch?v=j556MWGVVqI

88 For a discussion of the difference see: Hanh, T.N. (2008). *The Art of Power*. HarperOne.

89 See: *Vice*, Superstar Communist Slavoj Zizek is The Most Dangerous Philosopher in the West, (2013), https://www.youtube.com/watch?t=5m20s&v=XS_Lzo4S8lA&feature=youtu.be

90 This is a famous phrase drawn from a 1897 speech by German chancellor Bernhard von Bülow, which became synonymous with Germany's intentions, considered foolish by many contemporary observers, as well as, eventually, by Bülow's famed predecessor Otto von Bismarck, to build a vast overseas empire. See: Taylor, A.J.P. (1967). *Bismarck, The Man and the Statesman*. New York, Random House, Inc.

91 See paper: https://lifeitself.us/institute/equality-nationalism-power (forthcoming)

92 The tendency to like those who are similar to us is almost universal among humans, as detailed by academic research on homophily (love of the similar).

93 For another take on this issue see: Dougald Hine's piece on Alcoholics Anonymous for a whole culture, https://bellacaledonia.org.uk/2019/11/14/notes-from-underground-1-al-gore-didnt-want-you-to-panic/

94 See: https://lifeitself.us/institute/con-cit-sci/

95 For example: Kegan, Robert (1982). *The Evolving Self: Problem and Process in Human Development*. Cambridge, MA: Harvard University Press.

96 See: Thomas Hübl, Julie Jordan Avritt (2020) *Healing Collective Trauma*.

Liam Kavanagh is an embodied cognitive scientist, deeply influenced by Zen, who directs research at Life Itself, a community of people for a wiser, weller world. Past work in development economics convinced him that recognising and unlearning ideology is the most important step towards imagining futures worth creating. He helps create opportunities for this by organising residential learning communities, dialogues between Science and Zen, and contemplative activist groups.

CPSIA information can be obtained
at www.ICGtesting.com
Printed in the USA
BVHW041548150521
607436BV00007B/1666

9 781914 568022